The Many Dimensions of the Human Person

American University Studies

Series V
Philosophy
Vol. 96

PETER LANG
New York • Washington, D.C./Baltimore • Boston
Bern • Frankfurt am Main • Berlin • Vienna • Paris

E. Ecker Steger

The Many Dimensions of the Human Person

PETER LANG
New York • Washington, D.C./Baltimore • Boston
Bern • Frankfurt am Main • Berlin • Vienna • Paris

Library of Congress Cataloging-in-Publication Data

Steger, E. Ecker.
  The many dimensions of the human person / E. Ecker Steger.
  p. cm. — (American university studies. Series V, Philosophy ; vol. 96)
  Includes bibliographical references and index.
  1. Philosophical anthropology. I. Title. II. Series.
BD450.S74   1990, 1994   128—dc20   90–36346
ISBN 0-8204-1296-1   CIP
ISBN 0-8204-2568-0 (pbk)
ISSN 0739-6392

Die Deutsche Bibliothek-CIP-Einheitsaufnahme

Steger, E. Ecker.
  The many dimensions of the human person / E. Ecker Steger—
New York; Berlin; Bern; Frankfurt/M.; Paris; Wien: Lang, 1990, 1994
  (American university studies: Ser. 5, Philosophy; Vol. 96)
  ISBN 0-8204-1296-1
  ISBN 0-8204-2568-0 (pbk)
NE: American university studies/05

The paper in this book meets the guidelines for permanence and durability of the Committee on Production Guidelines for Book Longevity of the Council on Library Resources.

∞

© 2004, 1998, 1994, 1990 Peter Lang Publishing, Inc., New York

All rights reserved.
Reprint or reproduction, even partially, in all forms such as microfilm, xerography, microfiche, microcard, and offset strictly prohibited.

Printed in the United States of America.
Third Printing

To my three sons, Craig, Michael, and Sean,

who have made my life so rewarding.

Acknowledgments

For taking time from their own creative efforts to approve my book, I wish to express my indebtedness to my very good friend, Dr. John Rowan, renowned translator of St. Thomas Aquinas; to my former mentor, Dr. George McLean, Secretary-Treasurer of the International Society for Metaphysics, and my colleague, Father Robert E. Lauder, author of *God, Death, Art and Love,* a book on Ingmar Bergman. For assisting me in editing my book, I wish to thank Dr. Michael J. Heenan and for preparing the book for printing, my friend Ellen Hewitt. I am grateful for the sincere interest in my book shown by my students.

CONTENTS

Introduction	1
The Role of Being in Philosophical Anthropology	5
Chapter I. THE DIMENSION OF SELF	9
The Multiple Me's of Materialism	10
The Mind as Self According to Immaterialism	13
The Human Person According to Traditional Philosophy	15
The Unity of the Self	22
Dasein According to Contemporary Philosophy	25
The Self-Integration Process According to Jung	29
Summary	32
Chapter II. OUR SENSIST DIMENSION	39
What Can We Know According to Materialism?	39
What Can We Know According to Immaterialism?	43
The Sensist Dimension According to Traditional Philosophy and Biology	45
The Relation of World and Body According to Contemporary Philosophy	52
The Development of the Senses According to Piaget	54
Summary	59
Chapter III. THE DIMENSION OF UNDERSTANDING	63
The Falsity of the Understanding According to Materialism	63
The Dimension of Understanding According to Immaterialism	64
The Dimension of Understanding According to Traditional Philosophy	66
Differences in Operation of Sense and Intellectual Powers	71
Comparison Between Sense and Immaterial Ways of Knowing	72
What Is Thinking? According to Contemporary Philosophy	77
Summary	81

Chapter IV. THE DIMENSION OF WORLD   87

    A Materialist Environment   91
    The Ideal World of Immaterialism   97
    The World-View of Traditional Philosophy   101
    The Worlding of World According to Contemporary Philosophy 102
    Summary   106

Chapter V. DIMENSIONS OF FREEDOM, CREATIVITY,
        AND PLAY   111

    Is Freedom Possible in a Materialist Environment?   112
    Freedom as License According to Immaterialism   115
    The Dimension of Freedom According to Traditional Philosophy 118
    The Dimension of Freedom According to Contemporary Philosophy 124
    The Dimension of Creativity   128
    The Dimension of Play   132
    Summary on Freedom   134

Chapter VI. THE DIMENSION OF LOVE   139

    Love as Instinct According to Materialism   139
    The Idealization of Love According to Immaterialism   141
    Love of the Good According to Traditional Philosophy   145
    Love as a Coincidence of Opposites According to
        Contemporary Philosophy   149
    Summary   162

Chapter VII. THE DIMENSIONLESS DIMENSION   167

    The Meaning of Death   167
    The Dimension of Eternal Life   168
    The Relation of the Human Being to Being Itself   172
    A Frameless Framework   175
    Steps to Enlightenment   178
    The Dimensionless Dimension   182
Bibliography   191
Index   201

INTRODUCTION

In order to become aware of our many dimensions, it is necessary that we frame anew the question of the meaning of our being. A philosophical anthropology falls short of a discovery of what it means to be a human person if it is limited to a predetermined notion of man. To be open-minded to whatever can be uncovered in the way of truth in respect to man will enable us to discover the many dimensions of our being. Heidegger notes that whatever relates to the human person falls within the parameters of philosophical anthropology, which he defines as

> that interpretation of man which explains and evaluates whatever is, in its entirety, from the standpoint of man and in relation to man.[1]

Other philosophical anthropologies have closed the door to a deeper understanding of man by adopting restrictive methods of philosophizing, such as predetermining our way of being by the same method used for the positive sciences, i.e., reducing the human person to his physical components. Reductionism also occurs by limiting knowledge to sensations or its opposite, overemphasizing the role of reason rather than taking into account the whole person. Others overlook the ability of man to transcend his environment or turn attention away from the human person to the formal structure of speech. Philosophical anthropology does not fall within the parameters of the scientific method, yet many philosophers have entered philosophy through the door of science or mathematics, bringing with them the methodology appropriate only for their discipline. This is sometimes called the physicomorphic fallacy. It is true that both philosophical anthropology and science take their beginning from the observation of experiential data, but physics and mathematics, for example, measure their object in terms of discrete moments of time and space, breaking the whole into parts and then mechanically reconstructing them. On the other hand, philosophical anthropology begins with the experiential data of inner consciousness as well as external reality, leaving its subject matter intact. Henri Bergson points out that spatialized time, which is conceived in static moments by science and mathematics, is very different from the duration of inner consciousness which is the true apprehension of the nature of time. Reviewing Bergson, Collins states:

The spatialized time of positive science is composed of parts (points and lines), that are themselves immobile. Now from a combination of these *abstract, discrete immobilities,* it is impossible to reconstruct the *concrete, continuous, mobile* character of real duration. Hence there is a serious discrepancy between the mathematical time-factor, used in physics, and the enduring whole which we experience as our real temporal duration.[2]

Nor is psychology an adequate basis for a philosophical anthropology since, as William James notes, it is sufficient for that science merely to observe behavior rather than to understand that which makes a being to be. Since it is the study of a human being by a human being, a philosophical anthropology requires self-reflection as well as objective data. In Peirce's words, it could be said to be more of a Musement, a serious *playing around* with the possibilities of being. With our eyes open, we should awake to what is about or within us, opening conversation with ourselves. Meditation upon being will reveal the depth of its dimensions and will not only make us aware of ourselves but, according to Peirce, will inevitably suggest the hypothesis of God's reality.

Another limitation imposed upon philosophical anthropology is the reductionism favored by the sciences. The scientist Crick states that "the ultimate aim of the modern movement in biology is in fact to explain *all* biology in terms of physics and chemistry."[3] However, as Morowitz points out, reductionism must eventually lead to an epistemological circularity, since we begin with consciousness but must also end with consciousness, as the ultimate reality. For example, the mind is explained in terms of hormonal, neurological, and physiological components, and these physiological processes are in turn explained by biological structures; biological structures are then explained by atomic physics and atomic physics by quantum mechanics. But "quantum mechanics, in turn, must be formulated with the mind as a principle component of the system."[4] The Nobel Laureate Eugene Wigner agrees: "It was not possible to formulate the laws of quantum mechanics in a fully consistent way without reference to the consciousness."[5] One of the first scientists to see this with clarity was Heisenberg, who acknowledged with his

Introduction

indeterminacy principle, that the more accurately we know the location of a particle the less we know its momentum. We cannot *objectively* observe an incident as if we were completely external to it, but the external reality and the mind are inseparable. Many scientists have returned to the recognition that thought or mind is primary. Particularly in the study of the human person, it is necessary to consider the element of intentionality. Intention and attention permeate all facets of our being.

The belief that the ultimate explanation of all things is to be sought in its lowest components is criticized by eastern philosophers as naive and self-defeating. Suzuki notes that the oriental philosopher takes a holistic approach to his subject, studying it in its natural environment, leaving it intact. The problem of studying the human person piecemeal centers around the fallacy that a whole is merely a sum of its parts. An example of such a fallacy is the statement: This composition is excellent because each sentence is well written. Although adding to knowledge, reductionism, in itself, does not comprehend the many dimensions of the human person. To ascertain that which is unique about a human being, we must study him holistically.

In the wake of such branches of philosophy as logical positivism, linguistic analysis, and symbolic logic, attention has turned away from the human person to the analysis of the formal structure of speech. But in order to understand the human person, we need to decipher the experiences that are formulated in speech. Paul Ricoeur notes that, since our language has become so technical, we need to start again from the fullness of Being. "The first function of understanding is ... not attribution of predicates to logical subjects, but *pointing out, showing, manifestation.*[6] "The depth of human experience becomes manifest when speech returns to its roots in Being. Since Being is that which makes all things to appear - to shine forth - anything that places a limitation upon Being also deprives language of its ability to manifest. With the impoverishment of our understanding of what it means to be a human being, our ability to fulfill our many dimensions is also curtailed.

Another problem that must be addressed by philosophical anthropology is the limitation of the meaning of our being due to a closed epistemology. Whether it is sense knowledge or intellectual knowledge that is ruled out, the effect is a diminution of our possibilities. False criteria for truth can also curtail our knowledge of ourselves, e.g., accepting clear and distinct ideas as the only criterion for knowing reality. If the clarity of our ideas becomes a test of the real, then the unknown, e.g., the mystery of Being, must be excluded as unreal. By reflecting upon the limitations imposed by the presuppositions and methodology of a particular philosophical anthropology, we become more aware of the relation between its presuppositions and its derived tenets. This clearer insight helps us to avoid the limited vision that curtails the actuation of our many dimensions. In order to perceive this relation more clearly, a contrast will be made between various philosophical methods with the purpose of demonstrating differing ways of formulating worldviews. Taking a thematic approach to materialism and its opposite, immaterialism, it is demonstrated how these extremes fall short of a complete philosophical explanation of the human person. Other contradictories could have been chosen and would also have provided the same opposition with reconciliation by means of a coincidence of opposites. But since the period in which we live lays great emphasis upon the material, the opposition of materialism/immaterialism is chosen as most revealing.

Traditional philosophy not only offers an interesting account of the development of various philosophical ideas but serves as a reconciliation of the two extremes of materialism and immaterialism. As an extension to traditional philosophy, various contemporary philosophies, e.g., existentialism, will be presented - as a continuation of, as well as, in opposition to - traditional themes. In summary, this book presents a twofold approach, thematic and historical, as follows:

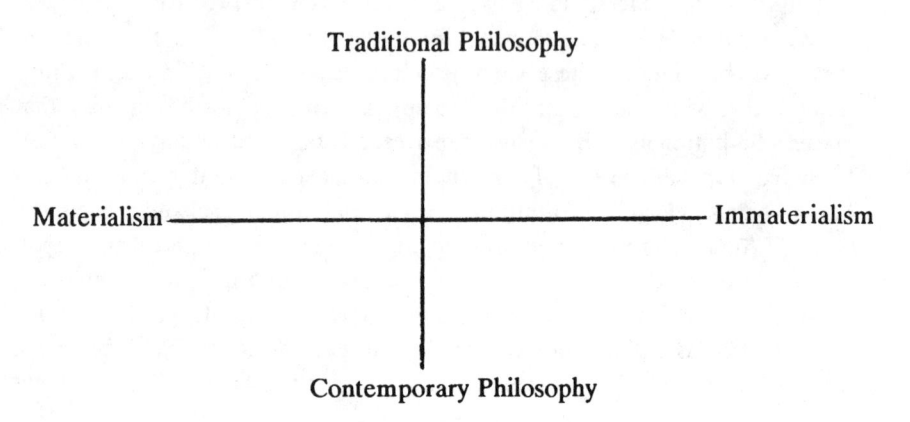

```
                    Traditional Philosophy
                            |
                            |
                            |
    Materialism ————————————+———————————— Immaterialism
                            |
                            |
                            |
                    Contemporary Philosophy
```

The Role of Being
in Philosophical Anthropology

Although it is imperative to avoid the aforementioned limitations, it would be impossible to have a completely presuppositionless philosophical anthropology. The question, *What does it mean to be a human being?* refers to the more primordial question, *What does it mean to be?* It presupposes therefore that the word *being* has meaning though just what this meaning consists of is left as an open question to be investigated. The question also presupposes that the word *meaning* has significance, implying that language enters into philosophical anthropology at the outset, yet at the same time denying that it usurps the role of Being. When Truth precedes Being, Being is limited to *being knowable*. But since Being is to a great extent shrouded in mystery, the question of Being should be left open in order that we can transcend our usual way of knowing and become increasingly attuned to Being. Because of the limitations of our intellectual power, anything beyond the reach of language transcends the parameters of intellectual competence. But since all that pertains to man falls within the context of philosophical anthropology, our investigations need not end with the rational; by using a phenomenological method, i.e., by a deciphering of the lived experiences of man, we can exceed the parameters of the problematic to encompass the dimension of mystery.

The mystery of Being is revealed only to Dasein. The human being is the only kind of being who stands consciously in relation to Being. Though many philosophers have found it easier to overlook the relation of man to Being rather than grapple with its complexity, it is this relation that distinguishes the human being from other forms of life.

In order to understand the uniqueness of the human being, it is essential that attention be given to the meaning of Being. The notion of Being defines the parameters of intellectual power and is the basis of truth, yet it is difficult to grasp. It is that which makes all Beings to be, yet it makes beings to be in different ways. Heidegger notes the all-embracing character of Being:

> Being is at once the emptiest and the richest...the most understandable and resisting of all conceptions...the most reliable and the most abysmal.[7]

In order to understand what it means to be a human being, it is necessary to differentiate the word *being* used as a substantive or noun, *being* used as a verb, *Being-in-totality* which includes both infinite and finite being and Being itself, which refers here to *infinite Being*. The word *being* in its noun form (without recognition of the verb form of being) merely points out an entity without in any way designating its existence. It is merely a label to refer to anything present in the environment.

The significance of the word *being* in its various verb forms (is, was, will be, can be, should be) is to point to *that by which* a being is or exists; it is that which makes us to be rather than not to be. We are beings (noun form) because of our act of being (verb form). This distinction is clarified by the following example: The word *meeting* can be understood as the presence together of several persons. In this case it is used as a substantive or noun. But the word *meeting* can also be used in its verb form to indicate the act of coming together, in which case it means the *coming together* of the meeting. It is due to the fact that there is a coming together (meeting as a verb) that a meeting (as a substantive) is able to be, i.e., if the persons did not come together there could be no meeting. Analogously, it is *being* that makes things to be. Just as we cannot speak of a meeting without considering that the meeting *meets*, to speak of beings without considering that beings *are* is to make a lifeless abstraction out of the word *being*.

The term *Being* when capitalized refers to both infinite and finite being, i.e. Being-in-totality. It is in the capacity of the human person to relate to Being-in-totality that Heidegger finds man's most unique way of being. The words *infinite Being* or *Being itself* denote the cause, unlimited itself, of all limited beings. Although many different names are given to infinite Being, this notion is present in almost all philosophies and religions the world over. Heidegger believes that the question of God cannot be answered until there is a clearer understanding of what is meant by the notion of God. Oriental philosophers, while implying a reference to Being itself, have refused to name

Introduction

the nameless *That*. The final chapter draws a comparison between eastern and western thinking in regard to man's relation to Being itself.

Since that which is unique about the human being is our mode of understanding ourselves in relation to Being, it is only by searching for and delineating this foundation of our being that we can bring to light its meaning and originate a valid philosophical anthropology. By reflecting upon our acts in the light of Being we are enabled to understand what it means to discover truth, to act in freedom, to be creative, to live authentically, and thus to realize our many dimensions.

In the various chapters, the following questions, as well as the question of being, are treated in a twofold way, thematically and historically: What is indicated by the notion of self? How do our senses help us to fulfill our material dimension? How does our understanding expand our horizon of being? What is the meaning of *world*? How does our relation to Being make possible our freedom? How can creativity enlarge our consciousness? How does the meaning that Being holds for us foster love, hope, and courage? And finally we ask the meta-question, What extra-ordinary meaning does infinite Being have for us as human beings? We seek the answer in both western and eastern thought and discover it in man's ability to transcend the being/non-being dichotomy to the dimensionless dimension.

1. Martin Heidegger, *The Question Concerning Technology*, trans. W. Lovitt (New York: Harper & Row, 1977), p. 133

2. James Collins, *A History of Modern European Philosophy* (Milwaukee: Bruce Publishing, 1961), p. 812

3. Francis Crick, *Of Molecules and Men* (Seattle: University of Washington Press, 1966), p. 10

4. Harold J. Morowitz, "Rediscovering the Mind," *Psychology Today* (August, 1980), Vol. 14, #3, p. 16

5. Ibid

6. Paul Ricoeur, "The Task of Hermeneutics," *Heidegger and Modern Philosophy*, ed. M. Murray (New Haven: Yale Univeristy Press, 1978), p. 155

7. Martin Heidegger, *Nietzsche*, 2 vols. (Pfullingen: Neske, 1961), II, 253

Chapter I

THE DIMENSION OF SELF

The contemporary world is undergoing a revolutionary crisis in which national interests are giving way to global reorganization. Now, more than ever, we need to tap the resources of the human person in order to meet this crisis armed with solutions that will foster international peace and community of interests. Do we possess capabilities of thought and action which we have not yet brought to fruition? If so, it is to our advantage to become aware of our many dimensions, so that we may live more personally fulfilling lives. Unless we draw upon our deepest resources, the problems now facing mankind cannot be solved. As a self, we each have a contribution to make which is vital to the well-being of the world community.

Recent discoveries have added an exciting store of information to perennial investigations of the nature of man. Yet many questions remain unanswered, e.g., Who or what is a human being, person, or self? Are we merely different in degree from animals, motivated by instinct and necessitated to act in a mechanistic way? Or does the human being possess powers which enable him to act freely and responsibly?

The question addressed in this chapter concerns whether or not there is a self and if so, what are its characteristics? In order to answer this question in a fundamental way, it is necessary that we understand the relation between the presuppositions of the particular philosophical anthropology and its necessarily derived conclusions. This relation will be considered in the light of various philosophies: first, the materialist notion which contends that there is no self but merely multiple states of consciousness; second, its opposite, that of immaterialism, in which the self is conceived solely as mind and its perceptions; third, as a reconciliation of the opposites of materialism and immaterialism, the traditional view of the human person as perceived objectively; fourth, traditional views are brought up-to-date by the notion of the human being as conceived by contemporary philosophy which studies Dasein (the human person) from the perspective of lived experience. The subject is thus approached thematically and historically throughout the various chapters.

The Multiple Me's
of Materialism

In considering the question of the self, it is important to study the presuppositions of the philosophy being considered. The materialist Hume (1711-1776) believes the only reliable knowledge to be sensations or a comparison of sensations which he calls ideas.[1] Only those impressions we receive from our senses can be used as evidence in defining a human being. Following from this presupposition, the question concerning man must necessarily be limited to: What do my senses tell me about man? Since only sensations are considered valid, Hume's answer to this question necessarily follows that man is merely a bundle of sense perceptions. Just as one would observe the qualities of a peach, e.g., that it is ripe, fuzzy, and round, man can be said to be nothing more than his physical qualities.

> As our idea of any body, a peach, for instance, is only that of a particular taste, colour, figure, size, consistence, etc. So our idea of any mind (brain), is only that of particular perceptions, without the notion of anything we call substance, either simple or compound.[2]

Materialism flatly denies any characteristics that would distinguish the human person from other beings or even from inanimate being. Hume explains that, if we were to subtract each and every physical quality possessed by a human being, there would be nothing remaining which we could call soul, substance, or self. Since a soul, substance, or self does not fall within the possibilities of sense perception, its existence must be denied. Does this mean, however, that if the self is not physical, it does not exist? Or, contrary to materialism, does the being of man, e.g., his personality, exceed the capacity of the sense knowing powers? Since the presupposition of materialism denies any knowledge other than sensations or a comparison of sensations, only the material dimension of man can be acknowledged.

Since, for Hume, there is no self or soul, there is no unifying principle by which the human being could be said to be the origin or source of his actions. How, then, does materialism define man? Hume says we are merely a multiple of different perceptions, following upon one another in rapid succession.

> The soul as far as we can conceive it is nothing but a system or train of different perceptions, those of heat and cold, love and anger, thoughts and sensations; all united together but without any perfect simplicity or identity.[3]

The empiricist William James further explains that our mind is nothing more than a *stream of consciousness* which consists of memories - some are dropped and some are added, e.g., abc, bcd, cde, def, and so forth. Since there are merely thoughts but no thinker, this *stream of consciousness* is held together by the *warmth and intimacy* one thought has for another. In the absence of such warmth, multiple personalities arise. James says: "The passing states of consciousness ... wander from duty letting large portions drop from out of their ken, and representing other portions wrong."[4] These are normal alterations of consciousness, but he also mentions three kinds of fractionated personalities: a radical change in personality, alternating personalities, and mediumships or possessions.[5]

As an empiricist, James believes that the person is not a single self but is many different beings which he calls the three Me's: the material Me, the social Me, and the spiritual Me. The material Me is made up of various layers: the innermost being the body, then clothing, our immediate family, our home, and possessions.[6] James considers the self-seeking material Me to act on instinct, e.g., "the tool-constructing instincts" or impulses to "hunting, the acquisitive, the home-constructing, self-seeking of the bodily kind," just as animals, without foresight, act on instinct.[7] Hume agrees. Experimental reasoning "which we possess in common with beasts, and on which the whole conduct of life depends is nothing but a species of instinct or mechanical power,"[8] In other words, for materialism, man is not capable of self-instigated action, but, like an animal, merely responds to whatever stimulates him the most at the time.

The social Me, according to James, consists of as many different images as there are persons who know me. Since the personality is fractionated with no identity or unity, "properly speaking, a man has as many social selves as there are individuals who recognize him and carry an image of him in their mind."[9] The social Me is dependent upon the recognition others give us, which, for materialism, consists of physical properties, e.g., one's actions and appearance, rather than intentions or character.

Rather than encouraging individuality, for materialism, conformity to social customs guarantees one's acceptability. Our sense of well-being is dependent upon the other's opinion of us.

> If every person we met were to *cut us dead* and acted as if we were non-existing things, a kind of rage or impotent despair would ere long well up in us, from which the cruelest bodily tortures would be a relief ....[10]

The loved one has certain attributes which are acceptable to the lover. If this collection fails of recognition, the loved one feels that *he is not*, since, "according to his own consciousness, he *is* not."[11] If we are merely a bundle of perceptions, as materialism contends, then the refusal of others to recognize this bundle will be our demise. However, if, contrary to materialism, our own self is the source of our being, then we can be self-reliant rather than look to others to bestow our worth upon us. Since approval of one's peers is of paramount importance for materialism, perceptions of the social self center around fame and honor, both of which make an impression upon *club opinion*. The psychologist Freud, who also is a materialist, has a similar notion - that the ego, rather than doing its own thinking, follows the example set by parents and society, internalized in an ego ideal. But does such conformity allow the individual to make his or her own independent judgments?

James says that it is easily seen that "the direct social self-seeking impulses are probably pure instincts."[12] Freud agrees. The id is the pleasure principle which pursues its own ends, with the ego in abeyance to its demands. We merely respond to a stimulus. Since materialism denies a self there can be no self-determination.

Since, for materialism, only the physical dimension can be perceived by the senses, the spiritual qualities of man are denied. As a psychologist who must use objective evidence, James says he cannot consider a *spiritual me*. But, as a philosopher, he denies that man is merely his physical properties. "The spiritual self is so supremely precious that, rather than lose it, a man ought to be willing to give up friends and good fame, and property and life itself." He calls the *spiritual me* the innermost core and the most important part of man. Our sensations are less intimate than our emotional desires and these are less intimate than our intellectual processes. Our volitional decisions are the most intimate and these "more *active-feeling* states of consciousness are thus the more central portions of the spiritual Me."[13]

In summary, because materialism accepts only sense impressions as valid, we cannot distinguish the human being from any other kind of being, e.g., a peach. Nor can we acknowledge a self. Our senses give us only discrete images and because each perception is discrete, we exist as a *bundle of perceptions* synchronized by our memory. As a collection of memories we cannot project ourselves into the future. And since there is no self, there can be neither independent judgment nor self-initiated action. Various theories of the human person consider, in a simplistic manner, man to be merely an accidental composite or bifurcate him into two different kinds of being so that his natural unity is destroyed. Are multiple personalities the natural state of the human person or is the self a unity? Although materialism contends that there are only multiple personalities, the opposite of materialism, i.e., immaterialism, posits a single self.

The Mind as Self
According to Immaterialism

For George Berkeley (1685-1753), who is representative of immaterialism, the self is a mind "which is a simple, undivided, active being."[14] Immaterialism thus appears to overcome the problem of multiple personalities. Since the mind is immaterial, it is not fractionated but is a single unit. Since Berkeley admits there are sensations, feelings, emotions, and other physical manifestations as well as thoughts, there seems to be no difference in the content of our being from that which we are accustomed to experience. We do our own thinking and are free to think as we will. However, does the unity of the self as posited by Berkeley allow for the power of will by which man acts existentially, i.e., in a real world? The theory of immaterialism has as its presupposition the idea that all is mind or the thoughts or sensations that minds perceive. For Berkeley, there is no world outside of mind. Since there is no external world causing our sensations, it is God who puts them into our mind. Berkeley proves his thesis, i.e., there is only mind, by referring to dreams.

> It is granted on all hands (and what happens in dreams, phrensies, and the like, puts it beyond dispute) that it is possible we might be affected with all the ideas we have now, although no bodies existed without, resembling them. Hence, it is evident the supposition of external bodies is not necessary for the producing our ideas, ...[15]

This seems to obliterate the distinction between dream and reality, but Berkeley considers the "dream to be shadowy and unclear compared to sense experience of real objects," i.e., those that are clear. It would appear to be an easy task to disprove Berkeley's thesis by stating that there is a real difference between imagining oneself burned and actually being so since the latter comes from an object external to the brain. However, Berkeley answers this by asking where it is that one experiences pain, in the object or in the mind?

According to Berkeley's epistemology, the question of the self would be posed: Since all is mind, what can the self do? The circularity of his reasoning is evident: the sole capacity of the self is to know, either by thinking independently or by receiving sense images from God. Does this mean that we make independent decisions and determine our own lives? At first sight it would appear so. However, although I may decide to do something, since it is God who is giving me my sense images, I cannot be said to have made the changes in the environment which, in turn, would cause an alteration of my sensations. The fact that I now see a house where there was none before cannot be due to my own work in building the house, since God alone is the cause of the sense impressions of the "real" house.

Since it is God who furnishes the sense images, is man responsible for his own product? If a man merely thinks he is building a house, yet he makes no change in his environment, is it he who is responsible for the weakness in its structure? It would seem that the responsibility for the house being well made or poorly made belongs to man rather than to God. However, according to Berkeley's theory, since our sense report comes from God and not from the external environment, the responsibility for a poorly constructed house cannot belong to man. Man is not even the secondary cause of the house that appears to the senses. The same holds for any act of doing or making. Although Berkeley contends that man has a will, he is unable to initiate any action in a real world.

Since all is mind, Berkeley can make no distinction between intentional and existential being. His theory, therefore, cannot account for a difference between thinking and willing. The basis for distinguishing thinking and willing, according to traditional philosophy, is that the former is intentional, i.e., in the mind only, whereas the action of the will ends in the world external to the mind, i.e., existentially. For example, with our intellectual power, we plan our actions and we use will power to put them into effect in a real world. But since there is no difference between external and internal reality for Berkeley, there can be no difference between willing and thinking. He admits this: "I find that I can excite ideas in my mind at pleasure, and vary and shift the scene as oft as I think fit." This is no more than willing.[16] Since willing and thinking are the same, although we might think we are acting, we are actually doing nothing more than thinking about it. The problem in this theory is that thought substitutes for action. Many persons lean toward immaterialism, demonstrating their idealism by devising innumerable plans but never putting them into action. Since the self is a thinker and not a doer, the planning of a paper suffices for the writing of it. Though the self is a single unit, it cannot initiate any action since its power to will is curtailed by sense images originated solely by God.

The Human Person
According to Traditional Philosophy

Traditional philosophy takes for its presupposition that, as a subject, we possess objective truth based on reason. The question following from this presupposition will be phrased: What can we know about man as viewed objectively? Is there a difference of kind between man and animal or is man merely a higher degree of the same species? Traditional philosophy sees clearly that, unless there is a clear distinction between man and other beings, there can be little understanding of the dimensions open to the self.

Unlike materialism, traditional philosophy finds, not merely a difference of *degree* between man and animal, but a difference of *kind*. By analogy, for example, a two ton truck is different in degree from a five ton truck. But a nuclear reactor has powers not possessed by a truck and is therefore different in kind. To ignore this distinction in kind makes it impossible to clarify whether or not there are powers belonging exclusively to the human person and, if so, what these powers are. If man and animal are to be differentiated, it will not be merely by a different degree of sensing capacity. For example, there is only one difference in the amino acids of the hemoglobin molecule between man and chimpanzee, less than between chimpanzee and gorilla. A difference of degree would mean that the animal could eventually be taught to take on the responsibilities of man. Since there is no evidence that an animal can think immaterially, it is this operation that is exclusively human.

Sensory power is always material, i.e., an image has reference to a particular time and space (this or that cup). The brain, for example, is a physical organ, and only physical realities are proportionate to it. Therefore, a power to be different will have to be immaterial, i.e., operating without reference to any particular time or space. Immaterial powers of intellect and will have proportionate to them immaterial objects such as justice, peace, and philosophy which are not extended and which therefore cannot be known by means of a sense image. Since no addition to a material dimension can turn it into an immaterial object, there must be a difference of kind between material and immaterial powers.

In order to better argue whether or not there is a difference of degree or kind between man and animal, it is essential to observe various axioms or first principles of reality. Although intellectually perceived, the axioms are derived from our sense experience of the real (extra-mental) world. The first axiom observes that in living beings there is a subject of every act which possesses various powers, enabling it to act upon a proportionate object:

Subject	Power	Action	Object
animal	*sense (brain)*	*producing an image*	*extended in space*

Note that the subject, power, action, and object must all agree in kind. The subject is determined to be an animal if its powers, actions, and objects all belong to the material dimension of the senses. In the example given above, materiality is present throughout - the material act of producing a material image of a material object denotes material brain power which defines the subject as a sensing being, i.e., an animal. A distinction must be made between power and action because one power can do many different actions. Further, a distinction must be made between power and subject since a power is sometimes actuated and sometimes not, but the subject must remain in act or it would not exist. There is a correlation between the subject, its powers, its actions, and the kind of object to which it relates. For example, an object proportionate to the sense appetite will be something sensibly agreeable rather than something immaterial, e.g., a bone, not philosophy, satisfies a dog's appetite.

The second axiom used to distinguish man from other beings is that we cannot attribute a power to a subject unless it demonstrates an action that corresponds to it. (We may perceive this action either through experience or by introspection). Why is this? Because if we did not hold to this axiom, philosophical anthropology would be about imaginary beings rather than about reality, e.g., contending that a dog can fly though we have never seen one doing it. Without this axiom, we could imagine any possibility and all properties would have to be attributed to every being. Any distinction between them would be lost. Since traditional philosophy is grounded in extra-mental being, it does not credit properties to a subject unless it demonstrates them. However, it has an open mind to whatever can be discovered and is ready to redefine a species whenever such a discovery is made, although having a record of being slow in appreciating new evidence.

A third axiom, which recognizes sameness in the universe, making it possible to preserve the continuity of life, is that the higher form always includes the lower. For example, communication is possible between animal and man only because man also possesses sense powers. If man were completely unique he would have nothing in common with other forms of life and could not live, e.g., breathe, in the same world with them. The following chart demonstrates how the human person includes chemical, vegetative, and sensitive life. Note that Berkeley breaks this rule by not positing the vegetative and chemical properties of man necessary to live in a real world.

A fourth axiom makes it possible to differentiate species. Since it is its most complex operation that distinguishes one species from another, to define the human person according to what he has in common with animals or plants would be to lose that which makes him unique. We do not say, for example, that because a child also uses a sensing language, man and animal are the same kind of being. If any human person is capable of an immaterial language not shared by animals, man must be credited with different kinds of powers. In the following chart it is clear that man could not be defined by the x but only by the #, denoting the immaterial powers which distinguish him from other kinds of being. Note that Hume breaks this rule by not crediting man with powers other than the senses.

immaterial powers				#
sensing powers			+	+
cellular		0	0	0
chemical	X	X	X	X
	non-living	vegetative	animal	human

A fifth axiom that helps us to avoid ambiguities and foster communication is that we should define or redefine our terms whenever necessary. Aristotle's definition of man as rational, for example, has lost its original meaning and is now used to indicate the behavior of animals. Other terms that are ambiguous are *abstract, instinct, generalization, analogy, language, reason,* and *learning,* since these words need the further distinguishing note of material vs. immaterial. Animals can abstract

The Dimension of Self

materially, but only a man can abstract immaterially, i.e., abstracting from the space and time of an object by which it is particularized. The same holds for all of the other above-mentioned words.

Tautologies provide no new information. To prove the immateriality of man's intellect by saying that it is not material is merely to repeat oneself by a circular argument. These axioms for right reason should enable us to make a valid distinction between man and other beings. In summary, they are as follows:

1. A subject is determined to be a certain kind of being, depending upon its powers, actions, and objects, all of which must be proportionate.

2. A power is not attributed to a subject unless a corresponding action is demonstrated.

3. The more complex form always includes the less complex forms of being.

4. The kind of species is determined by the most advanced action of its members.

✳ 5. Terms must be clarified and actions specified as to whether they indicate a material or immaterial operation. Tautologies do not provide new information.

Keeping these axioms for clear thinking in mind, let us examine the nature of man by first examining the most complex sensing operations of the higher animals and then comparing this activity with the immaterial operations of a human being to discover which of the following ways of defining man is correct:

I. Does man differ from an animal merely by a *degree* of sensing activity?
   OR
II. Does man, in addition, have different *kinds* of powers not possessed by animals?

The Smithsonian Institute of Washington, D.C. calls man the tool-making animal. However, gorillas have been known to strip a branch to make a tool to inject into an ant's nest. Nor can this be said to be merely an instinctive act on the part of the animal since a chimpanzee, though not previously experiencing the situation, was able to stack several boxes together to reach a banana. However, since these actions are material, they do not distinguish man from animal except by degree.

It is said that only a man plays, yet dolphins have been known to play ball with others of their species, sending such complicated messages as the particular location of the ball they are playing with. Dolphins are not only playful by nature but are show-offs, enjoying the feats they perform for their human spectators. They will also answer a call to lunch taped in their own language. It is important to note, however, although these are complex sensing operations, they are limited to communication about those objects or places that are material and extended, i.e., that exist in a particular time and space. *Come to lunch*, to a dolphin, means to move to a particular place at a particular time.

One of the most spectacular performances of animals is that of various chimps and gorillas who have learned to communicate with human beings. Using a computer console of seventy-five buttons, each bearing a symbol standing for a word, the chimpanzee Lana types messages for her trainer, Tim Gill. When Lana presses a button, a symbol is projected upon a display panel, enabling her to read what she has typed. Her trainer can communicate with her using the same symbols. Mr. Gill reports that

> if Lana presses the buttons for *Please, machine, give piece of apple,* a vending machine serves up a piece of apple. Lana can also ask for water, milk, the opening of a window, the playing of music or a movie from the *machine* .... One recent exchange involved a shoe that had been placed in a cardboard box. Mr. Gill asked where the shoe was and Lana said it was outside the box. Mr. Gill said no and Lana typed out, *Shoe is in.* Mr. Gill asked *Shoe is in what?* and Lana answered. *Shoe is in box.*[17]

It should be noted that all of the names Lana uses refer to concrete physical objects or actions, a place or time, or is conditioned, e.g., the button indicating *please* must be pressed before she receives a reward. With her senses she associates the object with the symbol. Lana can also disassociate an erroneous symbol projected upon the display panel and correct it with the appropriate symbol. In other words, her language consists of images of material objects or actions plus symbols to represent them.

A chimpanzee can not only send messages to a human being but can also use its language to speak to another chimpanzee, e.g., using a computer to ask for a tool. The only limit to animal language is that the operation must remain within the time and space dimension. He cannot understand something that cannot be sensed, such as the meaning of a thesis.

Teaching gorillas to communicate with American sign language is also effective, the gorillas not only addressing each other in the language but in one instance attempting, though unsuccessfully, to teach a cat how to sign. Spectacular as it is, however, gorilla language is limited to stringing together a sequence of labels, each of which is an association of a name with a sense image of an extended object, act, time, or place. Although an animal has coined many new words, they entail the association of several sense images. For example, water and bird were joined by a gorilla to form the new word "waterbird" to refer to a swan never seen before. Animal language, like all other actions of animals, are material sensing operations. An animal can also abstract as long as the abstraction remains on a material plane. Abstraction is generally defined as the ability to focus upon one part of a whole. For example, when a chimpanzee is shown one black and one white triangle and a black square, he can either point to the two black figures, ignoring the shape, or focus upon the two triangles, ignoring the color. This is a sensing operation since the color and shape of the object are determined by their extension in space and time. An animal has not been known to abstract immaterially, i.e., prescinding from all extension, such as knowing the meaning of philosophy which has no spatial dimension.

In summary, if an animal is able to abstract it is because the particular kind of abstraction concentrates on an extended property of an extended whole. If he is able to generalize, it is by means of the similarity of two or more physical objects. If he is able to see an analogous relationship, it is because it is a proportion of one material object to another. For example, chicks taught to ignore the lighter of two grains of corn and to peck at the darker one will strike at an orange kernel if placed with a yellow one, and yet ignore the same orange kernel and peck at a darker red one. As long as it is a comparison of physical objects or actions, the animal is capable of the operation. However, an animal cannot perceive an immaterial analogy such as: a biologist is to biology as a chemist is to chemistry. Nor can an animal abstract immaterially, generalize immaterially, nor understand the meaning of anything learned or known immaterially.

There is no evidence as yet that animal behavior demonstrates anything beyond sensing activity and, since every sensation is extended, a sensing being, i.e., an animal, is bound to the materiality of the sense world. But a human being performs operations not limited to a particular time and space and, therefore, a different kind of power must be attributed to him. Since a subject is determined to be a particular kind of being according to its powers, the human person is a different kind of being than an animal.

The Unity of the Self

To preserve the simplicity of the human person, we must reconcile multiple powers with the single self. Descartes, rather than positing a single self, divided the human person into two substances. Endeavoring to find a certain and reliable datum which would serve as a starting point for his philosophy, Descartes doubted the existence of all things including his own body. It was only his doubting mind that he could accept with certainty: "I think therefore I am." Descartes had to appeal to God for certitude that his sensations were not deceiving him - that he had a body - and thus created a hiatus between mind and body. Instead of a single self, he posited two unrelated substances, mind which thinks (mental thing) and body (extended thing) which he knew with certitude only through God. And, like Humpty Dumpty, they could not be put together again. Though Descartes attempted to explain the relation of mind and body through a pineal gland, since this gland is also physical, it could not unite with an immaterial mind any more than the body itself. Since that time, many philosophers have grappled with the problem of the unity of the human person. Some found the solution by settling for one half of man, either as mind, as in Berkeley's philosophy, or as body, as in Hume's.

Is there, according to traditional philosophy, a single unified self? Previous to Descartes, Thomas Aquinas (1224-1274) had already clarified the notion of the unity of the human person by positing, not two substances, but the co-principles of *esse* and essence which together make one being, e.g., just as the boundaries of an object do not make it into a second thing. It is *esse* that makes a being to be rather than not to be. Since our act of *esse* is one, we are one self.

We cannot create our own act of *esse*, i.e., we cannot make ourselves to be. Our initial act of *esse*, as well as any increment in being, is given to us by infinite Being. Finite beings possess *esse* whereas infinite Being is *esse* itself. There can only be one infinite. Therefore all other beings require a limitation of their *esse*. This limitation is called essence. The essence may be a material form (body) or an immaterial form (mind). Essence limits the *esse* of the person. This limitation or essence determines the kind of being, e.g., human being, animal, plant.

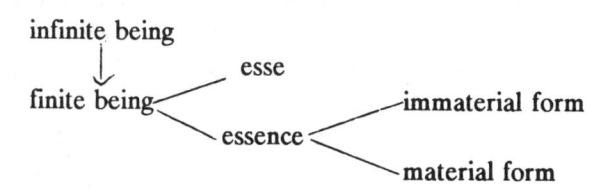

```
        infinite being
              ↓           esse
        finite being <           > immaterial form
                        essence <
                                 > material form
```

The co-principles, *esse* and essence, are not two substances, as in Descartes, but are two principles which coexist as one substance. In finite beings, neither *esse* nor essence can exist without the other. It requires *esse* to make one to be rather than not to be and it requires essence to limit one to be a human being. The mind is an immaterial form whereas the body is a material form occupying a particular time and space.

A single act of *esse* actuates our entire being in a dynamic unity of action, as follows:

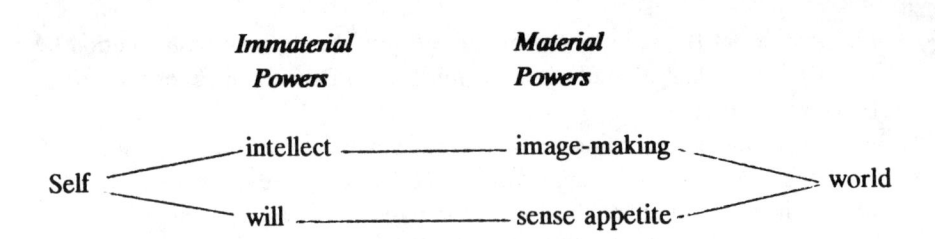

```
                Immaterial              Material
                 Powers                 Powers
                 ┌─ intellect ─────────── image-making ─┐
         Self ───┤                                      ├─── world
                 └─ will ──────────────── sense appetite ┘
```

Reading from left to right, Our self, actuated by infinite Being, in turn, actuates our immaterial powers of intellect and will insofar as we think and act. They, in turn, actuate our sense powers. Contrary to materialism, traditional philosophy contends that the senses of a human being are for the most part under the direction of the self.

Reading from right to left, our senses pick up data from the external world, making it possible for us to act within the limitations of time and space. They furnish the sensations necessary for the work of the immaterial powers, e.g., immaterial abstraction. The powers of intellect and will add being to the self. Although infinite Being is the primary cause, we enhance our self by acting as secondary causes, bringing about effects in the world, i.e., we increase ourselves in *esse* through the actions of thinking and loving.

We think with our power of intellect and love and act with our power of will. These two powers are distinguished by the fact that to know something is an intentional immanent action whereas loving is an *ecstasis*, a going out to the other as he is existentially. The intellect is moved by a formal cause (the known) and the will by a final cause (the good).[18] Since we possess more than one kind of power, we cannot identify with either one but must be the source from which these two powers spring; otherwise we would be a thinker but not an actor or an actor and not a thinker. Peirce equates the human person with his act of thinking, calling him a man-sign because we "*are* the symbols of our world-view." But this is to ignore the power of will in originating the symbols. Man not only thinks but possesses will power with which he directs his intellectual power to an end of his own choosing.

The human person actuates his own powers of intellect, will, and sense by drawing upon the power of the First Cause. Since we are secondary causes of our own action, we are autonomous and responsible. The difference between traditional philosophy's attitude about the relation of self to infinite Being can be summed up in the following: the materialist thinks, *The less to God. the more to man;* the immaterialist thinks, *The less to man, the more to God;* and the coincidence of these two opposites in traditional philosophy contends, *The more to man, the more to God.* The benevolence of God is demonstrated in the freedom and responsibility he has bestowed upon the human person.

Dasein According to Contemporary Philosophy

With contemporary philosophy the question of the self is no longer *What* is it? but *Who* is it? The self is not to be considered a thing among things but a way of existing. We cannot discover the meaning of our being by focusing upon our limitations as we would define an object. Whether or not we can be defined as a rational animal, a substance, a subject or an object cannot be decided before the question of what it means *to be* has been faced. "Dasein's Selfhood has been defined formally as a *way of existing,* and therefore not as an entity present-at-hand."[19]

The presupposition of contemporary philosophy is that knowledge of the human person should be derived from the principles of lived experience rather than from objective knowledge. It was Heidegger (1889-1976), who first drew attention to the necessity of defining *Dasein,* i.e., the human being, by emphasizing our relation to Being. This is to draw attention to our existence or *esse* rather than to our essence. "The question of existence never gets straightened out except through existing itself," says Heidegger, which means that it is not sufficient to define and explain *Dasein,* but that we must discover what it means to be through our own act of existing. It is only the human being who can question himself about Being, e.g., Why am I?, What is the meaning of my being?, and so forth. By drawing attention to the human person as *Dasein,* i.e., the one to whom Being presences itself, Heidegger sets the stage for the realization of the uniqueness of the human person.

The question of the self as posed by contemporary philosophy would be: What do the principles of lived experience point out about the human person (*Dasein*)? The answer to this question is sought by looking into the primordial state of *Dasein*. Heidegger notes that *Dasein* is always in-the-world-with-others. Whereas Descartes, through his methodological doubt, arrived at a thinking mind isolated from all others, he overlooked the fact that in order to doubt, he must doubt something. He failed to consider how he came to be aware that it was he who was doing the doubting. Hegel points out that I am not aware of myself except through the other - I am a being-for-itself only through another which is for-itself. Therefore the other penetrates me to the heart. For Descartes to eliminate all other beings by his methodological doubt would mean that he would not even know himself. The other is necessary for self-knowledge that *I am I*, since the other is the sounding board by which I become aware of myself. I cannot doubt him without doubting myself, says Hegel, since "self-consciousness is real only insofar as it recognizes its echo (and its reflection) in another."[20] Whether or not the awareness of the *I* requires self-reflection or is pre-reflective, as Sartre contends, it nevertheless remains that our awareness of the other is primordial to and the basis of our awareness of our own being. Relationship is not something added to our being. We are primordially in-the-midst-of-the-world with others. Heidegger emphasizes that the to- be of *Dasein* is a being-with, a *mit-sein*. He states:

> Not only is Being towards others an autonomous, irreducible relationship of Being: this relationship, as Being-with, is one which, with Dasein's Being, already is.[21]

By the word *primordial*, Heidegger means that which is prior to any consideration of any events occurring in the world. For example, the togetherness of Dasein in-the-world is prior to and necessary for a feeling of loneliness or withdrawal into self. This represents a radical rethinking of the notion of relation which in traditional philosophy is in the category of accident as added to the self. Relation is effectuated by empathy. By empathy, traditional philosophy means that we first understand ourselves and then, by identity with the other, sympathize with him. Heidegger, on the other hand, objects that, since we are initially with others, empathy denotes a prior alienation.

> Empathy does not first constitute Being-with: only on the basis of Being-with does *empathy* become possible: it gets its motivation from the unsociability of the dominant mode of Being-with.[22]

For example, Jung mentions a chieftain of a primitive tribe who, not yet being aware of his own identity, inquired of Jung why it was that, when he thought of doing something, his son did something different. The solution to his problem was not to feel empathy with his son but to distinguish himself from his offspring. The same problem is evident when parents refuse to allow their child to choose his or her own career. We are primordially with-others and must work to achieve an increasing independence.

How does our recognition of the autonomy of the self and of the other come about? There are two methods suggested depending upon whether the existentialism is negative (atheistic) or positive. An an example of the former, Sartre solved this problem by considering the other as a limitation of one's being.[23] One will not confuse himself with the other if he realizes the other is taking away his possibilities, e.g., a person peeking through a keyhole, enjoying himself until he realizes that someone down the hall is staring at him. We become aware of ourselves non-thematically through living the experience of the other's depriving us of our world. It is the other's look which manifests to us in shame or in pride that we are suddenly affected in our being and essential modifications appear in our structure. The other's look objectifies my subjectivity and gives me back to myself in shame. "Shame is shame of *self*; it is the *recognition* of the fact that I *am* indeed that object which the other is looking at and judging."[24]

To be thus looked at and judged strips us of our possibilities and thus denies our being, according to Sartre. Whatever possibilities I have are outstripped by the other's possibilities. Sartre gives an example of this: pursued by the other I hide in the corner. But the other takes away my possibility of hiding by shining a flashlight onto me. He has his hand in his pocket where he has a weapon. His finger is placed on the electric bell and ready at my slightest movement to call the police. My possibility of hiding is surpassed by his possibility of pulling me out of concealment, of arresting me.

> Once I am discovered in this cul-de-sac, I am caught ....
> Thus in the shock that seizes me when I apprehend the
> Other's look, this happens - that suddenly I experience a
> subtle alienation of all my possibilities ....[25]

In shame and anger and fear, I realize the other is the hidden death of my possibilities.

We are made aware that we are no longer master of the situation but have become enslaved by the values of the other. "In so far as I am the object of values which come to qualify me without my being able to act on this qualification or even to know it," says Sartre, "I am enslaved."[26] Insofar as I am constituted as a means to the other's ends of which I am ignorant - I am in danger.[27] Sartre considers this danger to be a permanent structure of our being-for-others.

Sartre sees with clarity that our existence takes on meaning only in relation to the being of the other. He realizes that the only way to escape solipsism is to reveal that the transcendental ego is primordially affected in its very being by other consciousnesses of the same type as man's. However, in disagreement with Sartre, is it apparent that we must be affected negatively by other consciousnesses? In contradistinction to Sartre's theory, we also have a non-thetic awareness of ourselves as separate from the other insofar as we realize his destiny differs from ours. In this event, the contrast is positive rather than negative. I come to the realization of myself as a being through the awareness of the other's act of forming his world in a way dissimilar to mine. I could not follow his destiny, nor he follow mine, yet both are acceptable and there is no alienation of either's possibilities.

We become aware of our self as we become more cognizant of our possibilities. Our destiny is our own concern, the openness of our being to others and to Being itself establishes the uniqueness of the self. Any definition of the self that misses this point leaves aside the most important dimension of our being. Since *Dasein* understands itself in terms of its existence, it becomes aware of itself by choosing whether to be itself or not to be itself. Our self comes to be through our choices. We need to discover whether or not it is we, ourselves, who have chosen these possibilities rather than letting others choose our way of being. Although we can let the *they* of publicness determine our existence and face our being as a *fait accompli*, each of us is responsible for what he makes of himself. Even if we neglect the question of our being, we are still a self who is coming-to-be, although in a deficient mode. Heidegger notes that it is only the particular Dasein which decides its existence, whether it does so by taking hold or by neglecting.

The Self-Transformation Process According to Jung

The psychologist Carl Jung perceives the self to be a coincidence of the opposites of conscious and unconscious. Jung believed the Freudian ego and id could be integrated into a higher self by means of a self-transformation process. Actions of the ego are typical of civilized man whereas actions motivated by the id are typical of primitive man. A coincidence of ego and id results in a self which, not only relates to the civilized world, but retains its intuitive roots. To effectuate the self-transformation process, Jung relies in part on dreams.

Analysis of dreams is not a recent phenomenon. Aristotle defined the dream as

> a presentation based on the movement of sense impressions, when such presentation occurs during sleep, taking sleep in the strict sense of the term.[28]

Aristotle points out that the dream can make us cognizant of the incipient stages of a disease.[29] It also can be predictive of events that will occur in the future. The dream serves as a token indicating a reality otherwise unrecognized by the ego. Just as we find that some actions we take during our waking hours cause the content of our dreams, so dreams can be cognate causes of the activities of our waking hours. This is readily seen in subliminal suggestion in which advertisements display symbols, not consciously visible, in an illicit attempt to sell products.

It may be a day or night dream or an intuition that draws our attention to a compensating factor to our conscious life that has been overlooked. Jung considers the dream to have personal validity as a symbol and an indispensable authority in the direction of one's life. It is

> a way of reflecting upon ourselves - a way of self-reflection
> .... It reflects not on the ego but on the self; it recollects
> that strange self, alien to the ego, which was ours from the
> beginning, the trunk from which the ego grew. It is alien to
> us because, through the aberrations of consciousness, we
> have alienated ourselves from it.[30]

The dream originates in the collective unconscious which is the inheritance, not of any particular culture, but of the human race, i.e., peoples of all races experience the archetypes of the collective unconscious. The dream has a content of its own which is not under our conscious control. It serves as a compensatory function to the conscious mind. Jung defines the dream as an "impartial spontaneous product of the unconscious psyche, outside the control of the will."[31] Dreams are helpful as an adjustment to a conscious attitude that is too extreme or misguided. They are

> therefore fitted, as nothing else is, to give us back an attitude
> that accords with our basic human nature when our
> consciousness has strayed too far from its foundations and
> run into an impasse.[32]

This is particularly true of a repetitive dream which, according to Jung, is trying to break through to consciousness but which is meeting some resistance from the ego.

Jung gives us a number of suggestions for the interpretation of dreams which provide us with insight into the self. He suggests that we treat every dream as though it were a totally unknown object and let our imagination play around with it. He objects that Freudian dream interpretation is too universal and that his materialist theory does not allow him to do justice to the "boundless freedom of the dream life." Although Freud contends that the sex instinct is not the only basis of dream interpretation, he equates a variety of objects with sexual symbols in a contrived correspondence, e.g., piano = hammers = box = female chest. His interpretation of dream symbols is not adaptable to individual differences. In contrast, Jung notes that the individual is the only one who can interpret his dreams, since it is only he who is aware of the significance the dream content has for him. Dreams would otherwise lose that virtue which makes them so valuable - their ability to offer the self new points of view. However, Jung suggests that it is beneficial to talk to others about our dreams, as they do in primitive tribes, since there may be material which our conscious mind is not ready to accept that others see more clearly. Freud and Jung agree that dreams are almost always about ourselves. The dream circumvents the unacceptibility of its material by presenting it as belonging to another person. If we dream of our father, mother, sister, brother, the dream is actually about that facet of our personality which is similar to the one dreamt about.

The dream compensates the conscious mind by making it aware of its potential and by correcting its attitudes. For example, a student who was afraid to take an examination dreamt that his friend, whom he considered to be much more intelligent than he, passed the same examination with a low mark whereas he passed with a high mark. He interpreted the dream to mean that he had underestimated his own capability and took the examination with confidence. In this case, as Aristotle suggests, the dream, by compensating his conscious ego, may have caused him to succeed. Jung suggests that a median between the conscious and the unconscious evaluations represents the best chance for a reconciliation of the two. Jung also believes that dreams can be prophetic.

Jung claims that in each of us there is another whom we do not know and who speaks to us in dreams. The collective unconscious is the seat of dreams. It is composed of archetypal figures representing universal characters such as anima, animus, wise old man, earth mother, and so forth. The wise old man gives advice in times of trouble. Jung claims that when

> we find ourselves in a difficult situation to which there is no solution, he can sometimes kindle a light that radically alters our attitude - the very attitude that led us into the difficult situation.[33]

Although Jung says that the self-integration process stems from our unconscious, it is necessary that the conscious mind become aware of what is taking place and take active steps to diminish the ego-centricsm that makes self-integration an impossibility. Our self is a personal unity, a unity of self-affirmation and self-negation. Unless we can say no to our most selfish desires we cannot hear the creative impulse of the collective unconscious.

Whereas Carl Jung pursues the question of the self from the motivation of the collective unconscious, Heidegger claims that our engagement in philosophy will codetermine the self we shall be. He notes that of which philosophy speaks should concern us personally, affect us and touch us in our very being. Contemporary philosophy points out that it is due to the relation of the self to Infinite Being that brings the self to awareness. To become aware of one's source of being allows one to draw strength from Being Itself. We are finite beings but have been given the power to act as secondary causes. But to recognize one's ability to act as a secondary cause, it is necessary to admit the primary cause which is the source of one's power. It is Being Itself which gives us our particular talents and in recognition of this gift we are responsible to develop these potencies. Christianity says that if God gives us five talents and we develop all of them, he will give us five talents more. Or if he gives us three and we develop three he will give us three more. But if we receive only one and we refuse to develop it we will loose even that one. Oriental philosophies often emphasize the here and now, thereby closing off a future too uncertain to contemplate. But Dasein considers not only the here and now but relates to the possibilities open to one in the future. Rather than fearing the future, it is possible to think, whatever I do I will give it my all to develop my talents in a way that is pleasing to Infinite Being. One solicits the attention of Being Itself as to what particular actions one should take to develop one's talents in order to make the most pleasing contribution. It is by turning one's attention away from the self and concentrating upon Being Itself that one achieves awareness of the role one is to accomplish. The self comes to be by relating closely to Infinite Being.

Summary

The difference among the three ways of perceiving the self is brought to our attention in contemporary philosophy's description of the mask or persona. Carl Jung and Gabriel Marcel describe three types of masks,

The Dimension of Self

corresponding to the notion of the self according to materialism and to immaterialism, the third type representing a coincidence of opposites as found in traditional and contemporary philosophy.

For the materialist, since there is no self, one's identity is dependent upon the mask that each person encountered offers him. According to Marcel, everyone is at times susceptible to the anguish of dependence upon another's opinion.

> This susceptibility is rooted in anguish rather than love .... The answer is that it is above all the experience of being torn by a contradiction between the all which I aspire to possess, to annex, or, still more absurd, to monopolize, and the obscure consciousness that after all I am nothing but an empty void; for, still, I can affirm nothing about myself which would be really myself; nothing, either, which would be permanent; nothing which would be secure against criticism and the passage of time. Hence the craving to be confirmed from outside, by another; this paradox, by virtue of which even the most self-centered among us look to others and only to others for his final investiture.[34]

The mask presented to the materialist by others is his only opportunity to confirm some semblance of a self.

The immaterialist, on the other hand, living in a world of thought, not limited by space and time, sees perfection within his grasp. Devising a mask of perfection, he then identifies with that mask. This may be a personal or religious idea of perfection or he may identify with an *ism* such as communism or any other *ideal* state or cult. He overlooks the fact that as limited beings we cannot expect to realistically identify with a perfect mask. Perfectionism, whether in a social form such as Hitler's Aryan race or on the part of the individual, is a mere abstraction. Such a person is *emptied out* into the mask and lives only the role. As Marcel comments, "He plays to the gallery; thinking that he performs for the other, he is really performing for himself." This *poseur* uses the other as a mirror to reflect back to himself the perfection that his mask requires of him.

> The *poseur* who seems only to be preoccupied with others is in reality entirely taken up with himself. Indeed, the person he is with only interests him in so far as he is likely to form a favorable picture of him which in turn he will receive back. The other person reflects him, returns to him this picture which he find so enchanting.[35]

But to use the other as a reflector is to treat him or her as an object rather than as a human being. To treat the other as a *useful good* is lacking in perfection. The more perfection we strive to achieve, the more likely we are to demonstrate our finiteness. To accept one's imperfections rather than to attempt to live an ideal image is more fitting for a being which is and always will be finite. We need to esteem our self even in the face of failure so that we are not tossed about with praise or condemnation. Nor should we empty ourselves out in a perfectionist role impossible to actuate in a real world.

In keeping with their notion of the self, traditional and contemporary philosophies believe the purpose of the mask is to meet the other halfway. We relate to the other first and foremost as a human being, but we assume an appropriate mask in our encounter with the other. We may, for example, wear professionally the mask of a professor but should be aware that the student is a human being with limited time, etc. In every walk of life a different mask is needed as appropriate behavior varies as one acts as son, employee, friend.

The presuppositions, questions, and conclusions concerning the self are as follows:

Materialism: Hume

> Presupposition: Only sensations have validity.
>
> Question: What can our senses tell us about man?
>
> Conclusion: Man is merely a bundle of perceptions, incapable of self-instigated action.

The Dimension of Self

Immaterialism: Berkerly

> Presupposition: There is mind only with its perceptions.
>
> Question: As mind only, what is a self?
>
> Conclusion: The self is the source of its thoughts but not the source of its sensations or actions.

Traditional Philosophy:

> Presupposition: Rational analysis gives us objective knowledge of man.
>
> Question: What is man?
>
> Conclusion: Man shares in the properties of the less complex forms of being but is different in kind since he possesses immaterial powers.

Contemporary Philosophy

> Presupposition: The principles of my lived experience reveal my relation to Being.
>
> Question: What do the principles of my lived experience reveal about the being of Dasein?
>
> Conclusion: Dasein (man) is the one to whom Being communicates itself (only Dasein questions his own being, e.g., why he is, who he is, and so forth).

1. David Hume, *Enquiry Concerning Human Understanding from The Essential Works of David Hume*, ed. R. Cohen (New York: Bantam Books, 1965), p.51

2. Ibid., p. 544. Author's parenthesis added.

3. Ibid., pp. 543-44

4. William James, *Psychology: Briefer Course* (New York: Collier Books, 1962), p. 216

5. Ibid., pp. 218-221. Fractionated personalities occur when there is a radical change in the personality, e.g., an adolescent, wishing to impress his peer group with his self-sufficiency, rejects a demonstration of parental love. James says this is not to be considered pathological unless there is an irreconcilable contradiction between the two personalities. In pathological cases the patient may be alienated from his body, hear voices that *make* up his mind for him, and even feel he no longer exists. The second kind is alternating personalities. The subject may be hypnotized and if told to forget all that has happened to him and that he is another person altogether, *he throws himself into the new character with a vivacity proportionate to the amount of histrionic imagination which he possesses.* In pathological cases the transformation is spontaneous. The third kind that James mentions is mediumships or possessions such as trance states which the person deliberately solicits. Since the language used by mediums during their trance is uncannily similar, James believed mediums tap into a strata which he called the Zeitgeist. Other paranormal experiences have been studied by James and have been found to be genuine, although escaping the criteria for valid scientific data, e.g., clairvoyance, pre-cognition, telepathy, and psycho-kinesis. Animals, also, have been known to have extrasensory perception and it is assumed that the above listed phenomena belong to the material dimension. The relation of paranormal experiences to the self remains an unsolved problem. Do split-off personalities argue against a single self or do they represent a generally unrecognized capacity of a single self? Without self-identity we could not be aware of a trance state as a possession but would identify with each alternating state.

6. Ibid

7. Ibid., p. 196

8. Hume, *Enquiry* ... , p. 123

9. James, *Psychology* ... , p. 192

10. Ibid., p. 192

11. Ibid., p. 193

12. Ibid., p. 197

13. Ibid., p. 194

14. George Berkeley, *A Treatise Concerning the Principles of Human Knowledge,* ed. T. E. Jessop, *The Works of George Berkeley,* (London: Thomas Nelson & Sons, 1964) II, 138

15. Berkeley, *A Treatise* ..., II, 48

16. Ibid., p. 139

17. Boyce Rensberger, "Talking Chimpanzee Asks for Names of Things Now," Copyrighted 1974 by *The New York Times* Company. Reprinted by permission

18. Thomas Aquinas, *Summa Theologica* I-II, 9, 1; I, 59, 2, ad 2

19. Martin Heidegger, *Being and Time,* trans. J. Macquarrie & E. Robinson (Oxford: Basil Blackwell, 1967), p. 312

20. Georg W. F. Hegel, *Propedeutik,* first edition of his complete works, p. 20

21. Heidegger, *Being and Time,* p. 162

22. Ibid.

23. Jean-Paul Sartre, *Being and Nothingness*, trans. H. E. Barnes (New York: Philosophical Library, 1956), p. 251

24. Ibid. p. 261

25. Ibid., pp. 264-265

26. Ibid., p. 267

27. Ibid., p. 268

28. Aristotle, "De Somniis," *The Basic Works of Aristotle*, ed. R. McKeon (New York: Random House, 1941), p. 625, 462a30

29. Aristotle, "De Divinatione per Somnum," *Basic Works*, p. 463, 312a20

30. Carl Jung, *Civilization in Transition*, in *The Collected Works of C. G. Jung*, trans. R. Hull, 10 vols. (New York: Pantheon Books, 1964), X, 149

31. Ibid.

32. Ibid.

33. Ibid., p. 153

34. Gabriel Marcel, *Homo Viator*, trans. E. Crauford (New York: Harper & Row, 1965), p. 16

35. Ibid., p. 17

Chapter II

OUR SENSIST DIMENSION

How can our sensist dimension contribute to the unfolding of the self? What are the possibilities and limitations of our sensory powers? What is the criterion that determines whether or not sense perception corresponds to a real world? A philosophical anthropology should provide a comprehensive theory of sensation. Can a materialist or an immaterialist philosophy give us knowledge of reality? Finally, what does traditional and contemporary philosophy and psychology contribute to our understanding of sensation?

What Can We Know According to Materialism?

For materialism, knowledge consists solely of sensations. According to David Hume, ideas are nothing but copies of sense impressions "which remain after the impression ceases and this we call an idea."

> All our ideas are nothing but *copies* of our impressions or, in other words, that it is impossible for us to *think* of any thing which we have not antecedently felt.[1]

Since the original sensation and the subsequent *ideas* (comparison of sense images) are equally the product of the senses, Hume is only able to account for our material dimension. This would indicate that our sensing operation differs from that of an animal merely by degree.

According to Hume, since thinking is difficult and often in error, we should rely on our senses which he believed to be infallible. But he did not consider, since our senses are not aware of how they produce an image, we would not know if they were in error. Hume, himself, states that this mechanical power "acts in us unknown to ourselves." The external senses cannot self-reflect, e.g., the eye cannot see itself seeing. And though the internal senses have a mirror-like repetition at the edges of the various areas of the brain and so could be said to reflect, they cannot self-reflect. Since images appear to us complete, we are not aware of our part in forming images. Consequently, we cannot say if our brain has formed them correctly or not. We can know, however, if we have correctly associated one image with another, the sound cup with the visual image of a cup. Though Hume believed the senses to be always correct, he overlooked the possibility of the senses mismatching words with sounds, e.g., using the word *apple* to indicate a banana. Such an error is easily noted even by a chimpanzee.

In invalidating intellectual knowledge, materialism destroys the possibility of demonstrating that sensations are valid representations of a real world. With no notion of real causality, Hume cannot substantiate a necessary connection between the material form of the extra-mental reality and the image. He says that we cannot be certain that what is sensed is there at all. We can only be certain of the sense impression - the ultimate cause of sense impressions is perfectly inexplicable by human reason. He asks the question: How is it to be determined whether sense perceptions are produced by external objects and then typically appeals to sense knowledge, rather than intellectual knowledge, for an answer:

> But here experience is, and must be entirely silent. The mind (brain) has never any thing present to it but the perceptions, and cannot possibly reach any experience of their connexion with objects. The supposition of such a connexion is, therefore, without any foundation in reasoning.[2]

Hume failed to note that as we compare one sense image with another we relate our sensations to the activities of our body. For example, we can make a pencil, held close to our face, appear smaller by moving it at arm's length. Since this occurs every time, we become aware of distance as a determining factor in our sensations. Also, we observe that our image changes with the light that is reflecting off the pencil. Although the sense image is produced by our brain, the cause of these variations are necessarily from the external object. But, since it requires an intellectual power to understand the idea of a necessary connection between the object and the sensation, Hume was unable to explain how a sense image comes to be.

Even his suggestion that perhaps sense images "are deriv'd from the author of our being" cannot be admitted, since the "author of our being" could not be known by the senses. To appeal to God for the derivation of our sense images is very close to Berkeley's immaterialism. And like its opposite, materialism is unable to substantiate a world external to sense perception.

Since, for Hume, there is no reality evidenced by sensations, how does he account for a difference between real and imaginary sense images? Traditional philosophy points out that sense images of the real world are a product of the brain limited by the material form of the existent. Because we are aware of alterations in the reception of light, sound, or some other physical medium, we know that the material form of the image, its shape, size, color, and so forth is from an object external to the brain. On the other hand, we realize that the material form of an imaginary image is not being received by our external senses, but various sense images are recalled by the brain and joined together to make a new image, e.g., a flying horse. But since Hume cannot prove that sensations receive their material form from the external world, he has difficulty knowing which are real and which are merely imaginary. He must therefore devise some way of distinguishing them. Sensations of what we call real, Hume says, are lively and strong, whereas comparative sensations, which he calls ideas, thoughts, or experimental reasoning, are weaker sensations. Since he cannot prove an external world, Hume, like Berkeley, must depend upon the clarity of his knowledge to distinguish what is real from what is unreal. The fallacy of this is evident: I have a clear image of the building I wish to build though it is as yet non-existent. But, according to Hume, since it is a clear perception, the building must be real rather than imaginary. On a foggy dark night, my sensations of reality are very unclear, whereas, for Hume, the foggy dark night must be unreal. With the distinction, clear equals real and unclear equals imaginary, materialism and immaterialism find themselves agreeing. Although at opposite poles in respect to their presuppositions, these two extreme philosophies are faced with the same inability to make a valid distinction between idea and reality.

Hume thought his greatest contribution to philosophy was his understanding of the operation of the senses. He extols the imagination as the greatest power man possesses.

> Nothing is more free than the imagination of man; and though it cannot exceed that original stock of ideas, furnished

> by the internal and external senses, it has unlimited powers
> of mixing, compounding, separating, and dividing these ideas,
> in all the varieties of fiction and vision.[3]

In spite of the richness of our imagination, as Hume himself notes, it is limited to the space/time continuum.

> This creative power of the mind (brain) amounts to no more
> than the faculty of compounding, transposing, augmenting, or
> diminishing the material afforded us by the senses and
> experience.[4]

This power is limited since images can be combined and rearranged within space and time but cannot transcend space and time, i.e., since images have to be known by a brain which is also extended. For example, although we can imagine a red box sitting on top of the desk, we cannot imagine a red box and a blue box of the exact size sitting in the same place at the same time. Since two extended objects cannot occupy the same time and space, neither can two images, since they, too, are extended.

Hume's greatest contribution to philosophy, as he himself states, are the principles of the association of ideas (sense images). There are four principles which regulate the sensing operation, viz., Resemblance, Association, Contiguity, and Causation.[5]

Resemblance or similarity is the association of two or more things that are alike in appearance. This principle makes it possible for the senses to generalize as long as there is a physical similarity. An animal, for example, can generalize from one to many variously shaped cups as long as the gap between the appearance of one and the other is not too great. This capability on the part of the senses does not extend to immaterial generalizations such as knowing physics, chemistry, and so forth as sciences.

The principle of association refers to two things that are dissimilar but are introduced together such as the sound cup and the visual cup. Hume says that if we see a picture of an absent friend, every passion which that idea occasions, whether of joy or sorrow, acquires new force and vigor. He cites the ceremonies of the Roman Catholic religion as that superstition which enlivens devotion through the association with physical objects, "which otherwise would decay if directed toward distant and immaterial objects." He does not see the material object as a symbol of the immaterial or spiritual appreciation of God but as the worship of an idol. Hume says the difference between fiction and belief is merely a matter of sentiment which cannot be commanded by the will.

The principle of contiguity in time enables the brain to relate the notes of a melody played one after another. Contiguity in space refers to anything side by side to another physical object.

Hume's principle of causation might better be called pseudo-causality since it is the sense perception of a prior and posterior order of events without a necessary connection between them. Hume gives the example: when he throws a piece of dry wood into a fire, it augments the flame. But this transition proceeds, not from reasoning from a cause to its effect, but its origin is altogether from custom and experience. There is only a present object (the fire) and a customary transition to the increased flame which is conjoined to the fire.

These principles are equally applicable to man and animal since they are purely sensing activities. They depend upon probability rather than upon human design. Although Hume analyzes carefully the operation of the senses, he does not acknowledge the selective role which we, with our immaterial powers, exercise upon them. He thus misses the uniqueness of human sensory activity, equating it with that of an animal.

What Can We Know According to Immaterialism?

According to Berkeley, all is mind. Man does his own thinking, but sense images are put into his mind by God.[6] Sensations are distinguished from thinking by their clarity and make up what we call reality, i.e., *real things* are sense impressions whereas thoughts are not as clear. With no real world Berkeley, like Hume, must resort to a theory of knowledge which makes the distinction: clear equals real, unclear equals unreal.

Berkeley's idea that our images are imprinted on our senses by God is contradictory since an immaterial mind cannot be imprinted with sensations which are material, i.e., having extension in time and space. Since, for Berkeley, immaterial minds are the only reality, we have no brain either to produce or preserve images. How then can an immaterial power be made to receive sensations which require a material, extended organ in order to be? Berkeley answers this objection by saying that "it no more follows that the soul or mind is extended because extension exists in it alone than it is red or blue....."[7] Although it is true that the mode of a sensation is different from that of the object, the brain, nevertheless, must retain in its own extended manner the particular color, shape, and other qualities of the object since, if the particularity of the image is lost, it could never be recalled. That sensations require an extended brain is evident, since the color a person is looking at alters his brain wave tracings. Perceptions of red, green, and yellow light, as well as of shapes such as squares and circles, all have their own characteristic tracings and these tracings are essentially the same from person to person. The brain in its own manner becomes that which it perceives and, since that which it perceives is extended, its tracings, too, must be extended in order that the image is not merely *about* a color or shape but *is* a particular color or shape. For example, the color red can be known by an immaterial mind as a breakdown of white light into red and its opposite green. However, for a congenitally blind person, this would not offer an *experience* of the color red but merely be *about* the color red.

Another problem with Berkeley's thesis, i.e., that God puts sense images into our mind, is, that if our senses are merely receptive of whatever God wishes to give us in the way of sensations, we would not be able to bring about our own effects, e.g., it would not be our decision as to what color we painted the table. Nor could we focus our attention on the particular sense data we found to be relevant in planning an undertaking. Although Berkeley says that the mind is active, since the self does not create its own effects, it would be completely passive to its reception of sense images. Nor could there be interaction between thought and sensation if the latter were totally caused by God. We could not be held responsible for the quality of an object if we are receiving our sense report, not from the object we supposedly created, but from God.

Although of opposing philosophies, neither Berkeley nor Hume could admit the reality nor the causality of the external world. The only way either could be aware of a so-called real world is by the clarity of their sense impressions. But an epistemology based on clarity of ideas does not allow for the unexplained mystery of Being which is more real than our clearest sense impressions. Neither an overemphasis upon mind, as in immaterialism, nor upon the senses, as in materialism, can substantiate the reality of our world, nor even account for the sensations themselves. We turn, then, to traditional philosophy for an explanation of sensing activity with supplemental material from current biological research.

The Sensist Dimension According to Traditional Philosophy and Biology

According to traditional philosophy, for the most part our immaterial powers direct our sense powers. Through attention and intention, we direct our senses to selected data and, in turn, our senses furnish our immaterial powers with images of the external environment. Unlike man, an animal directs its gaze to those objects which are instinctively proportionate to it. A frog, for example, will strike at any moving object that conforms to his appetite. It can starve with dead flies within its reach since his eye is geared only to those edible objects that are in motion. However, the human being directs his own sense operation according to the attention he wishes to focus upon various ends of his own choosing.

How do our images come to be, according to traditional philosophy? Just as we require two co-principles to explain that a human being is and is limited (*esse* and essence respectively), an image must also be constituted by *esse* and essence. Our brain creates the *esse* of the image, making it to be. The image is limited by the essence (material form) of the object. Hence, the image *is* because the brain created it, but it is an image of the box because we have received the material form of the external box.

We receive the material form of the object through our external senses. Physical media, such as light waves, bounce off the object, carrying its material form to the eye. The shape of the box, causes the light to reflect the edges of the box, revealing its particular size, shape, color, texture, and so forth. It is not the *esse*, i.e., the real being of the object that is conducted to the brain but the limit of the object. Its material form limits the image the brain creates, making it a likeness of the external object. Analogously, like making a popsicle, the mold or material form comes from the external object, and the brain furnishes the juice to fill the mold.

There are two principles at work: the brain creates the *esse* of the image making it to be and the material form of the object limits the *esse* to be like itself. Since it is our brain that creates the *esse* of the image, our knowledge is our own. Because the material form of the object limits the *esse* of the image, making the image to conform to it, sense knowledge is a valid representation of the external world. There is a necessary connection between the external object and the brain, since without the brain there could be no image, and without the material form of the object the image could not be a likeness of the external reality.

The sensing operation is material throughout. A physical medium is required to carry the form to the eye, ear, or some other external sense. The form is then transferred by neurons to the brain. Since the neurons that relay the visual sensation to the brain are the same as the neurons that relay the auditory sensations, visual images are differentiated from auditory images by being received in different parts of the brain. Various areas of the brain are empowered to handle specific operations, the complex human brain having probably somewhere between fifty and one hundred discrete areas. Although each area has a fairly well-defined boundary, mapping is difficult since the areas interact at their edges with a mirror-like repetition. The form of the material object, the medium that transmits the form, the external sense organ receiving the form, the neurons, the chemical synapse, the electromagnetic waves and sound waves present in the brain, as well as the brain itself, are all material, i.e., extended in time and space, and therefore different from an immaterial operation.

Although there is still insufficient data to support any complete theory of the brain, contemporary research reveals something of its structure. The human brain is a combination of precision wiring and associative nets. Using a magnetoencephalogram (MEG) the magnetic field of the brain can be detected and the movement of ions into and out of brain cells can be detailed without interference with the brain's activity. With this method it is perceived that stimulation of various parts of the body produces a corresponding activity

Our Sensist Dimension 47

in a particular region of the brain, demonstrating that the coherence between the two is dependent upon the space/time continuum.

With our internal senses we unite the data of the external senses. The sound issuing from a television set, for example, is synchronized by our brain with the visual image. As the empiricist William James notes:

> Any number of impressions, from any number of sensory sources, falling simultaneously on a mind (brain) *which has not yet experienced them separately*, will yield a single undivided object to that mind (brain).[8]

The uniting of the sense data is limited to the kind of unity present in the external environment. Because the sound and light waves of a television set issue from the same space and time, they will be joined as one by the brain (Principle of Association). If the kind of unity is not material it will escape the senses, e.g., the unity of a political party, which is dependent, not upon the members being physically present together, but upon having the same immaterial ideas.

The brain acts as a storehouse of memories. Brain wave tracings are preserved in short term memory and by repetition in long term memory. The internal senses have the ability to store images and later to break them down into their component parts. The straight lines of artifacts and the curved lines discovered in nature furnish the imagination with the basic forms necessary to create a myriad of new images. Most of the work of the imagination is under the direction of the immaterial intellectual power. We create appropriate sense images to illustrate our thoughts. Arnheim points out that many of these *mental images* are incomplete as compared to brute sense images, e.g., a scale as an illustration of justice.[9] The thought has a more precise content than the image which merely serves to illustrate what otherwise would not be as concrete and easily understood. The process is highly selective. The image does not merely *copy* the external object but points out the object's most salient points. Arnheim quoting Tichener says:

> that the incompleteness of the mental image is not simply a matter of fragmentation or insufficient apprehension but a

> positive quality, which distinguishes the mental grasp of an
> object from the physical nature of that object itself.[10]

Although the image illustrates an idea conceived by our immaterial power, since our senses are subject to the limitations of time and space, they cannot furnish an exact portrayal of that which is being considered. The usefulness of the senses depends upon their ability to suggest rather than to copy the actual object. Arnheim says:

> It offers the possibility of reducing a theme visually to a skeleton of essential dynamic features, none of which is a tangible part of the actual object.[11]

Picasso's interesting study of a bull in which, in a number of different drawings, he increasingly reduces a realistic portrayal of the bull to its essential form, is a good example of how he used his intellectual intuition to direct the work of his senses.

Another area of our brain which coordinates sensations within the limitations of time and space is the limbic area. We receive impressions, e.g., of pain or illness, and transmit messages to the various parts of our body. In one case a patient was unable to receive incoming messages and did not know the position of his body. Since he retained his ability to send messages to his extremities, he was partially able to overcome this deficiency. By looking to see where his feet were located, he was able to walk. When covered by a blanket, however, he could not move. Unless incapacitated, the brain, taking its direction from the immaterial powers, provides the means whereby the actions of our body are directed toward a goal.

Split-brain experimentation reveals that the right and left hemispheres have different functions.[12] The left hemisphere contains the speech center for right-handed persons, although for persons who are naturally left-handed this will be reversed. Some experiments have demonstrated that the left hemisphere tends to be the dominant one and will direct the right hemisphere by force if necessary. In one instance a patient raised his left hand (directed by his right hemisphere) to strike his doctor, but his right hand intercepted the attack.

The right hemisphere provides the sensing part of creative effort and is adept at spatial manipulation such as working a jig-saw puzzle. Recognition of a face takes place in the right hemisphere, whereas the name associated with the face is recalled by the left hemisphere. As the creative center, the right hemisphere has a global approach. Right hemisphere damage may give rise to inappropriate emotional behavior and impair recognition of emotion in others. A patient may still be able to understand what is said but does not grasp the emotional tone, failing to recognize, for example, whether it is said in an angry or a humorous way.

It is generally believed that the speech center is the only hemisphere capable of language. However, the right hemisphere is capable of a rudimentary type of language such as combining the sound of a word with an image. Although the right hemisphere is incapable of oral speech, it can arrange letters to form simple words such as nouns. This has proven helpful to patients with paralysis of the left hemisphere.

Without a stimulating environment in his early years, a human being cannot fully learn to speak a human language. In southern France, a so-called wild child, abandoned in the forest many years before, was discovered by a farmer. The boy was attracted to the bonfire where the farmer was cooking potatoes. The child reached into the hot coals to grab the potatoes without any sense of pain. He emitted only growling noises and seemed oblivious to those around him. Since he did not respond to anyone speaking to him, he was thought to be deaf and was placed in a home for deaf mutes. However, his teacher discovered that the boy immediately reacted to the sound of nuts being cracked. The teacher then tried to teach the boy to speak. His right hemisphere progressed well and he was able to match written words with objects and to say the word *water*. He seemed to have the resources of a human being, spending hours in thoughtful concentration whenever he was reminded of his former life. When it rained or snow fell, he would look out of his window and contemplate the scenery. But though he progressed very steadily, he was unable to grasp left hemisphere language and many years later still had no capability of expressing himself verbally. Like animal language, his vocabulary was generally limited to right hemisphere language, i.e., sense images plus a written word. His language remained retarded despite the concerted effort of his teacher.

This would indicate that if the environment is too limited at an early age the material dimension of a human being will suffer consequent impoverishment. This is also true of animals. White-crowned sparrow chicks, for example, must hear their species' song between the 10th and 50th day of life or they cannot *tape* and store the parental songs in the brain. There is also some evidence that infants respond to many more consonants than are used in their parent's language and that hearing a foreign language, even though not understanding it, enables the child to later speak it without an accent. This ability disappears by the time the child enters school.

In order to fully develop the senses it is necessary to increase our awareness of the external world. Our environment becomes the richer the more we train our senses to discriminate accurately. An example of the necessity of such development is made evident in the following incident: two children raised by blind parents were discovered to move about their house by touch. Although they had good eyesight, they had not learned to use their eyes. When placed in a school with other children, they began to see. In a similar way, we learn to appreciate classical music and fine art by exposing ourselves to it. Appreciation of music begins in the right hemisphere but changes to the left hemisphere as appreciation is fostered.

Anxiety or boredom is often compensated for by overuse of a sense such as the taste for food. Excess is harmful for the senses. For example, overeating causes the body to overwork itself, e.g., each pound of excess fat requires two hundred miles of capillaries.[13] Loud music can harm the delicate eardrums causing deafness in later years. Damage to the brain through use of narcotics is irreparable since it breaks down the nucleus of the brain cells. All stimulants are potentially addictive since they activate the pleasure center of the dopamine circuit. Narcotics, unlike food, do not reach a level of satiation and addicts will use whatever means to attain a drug. Alcohol and other depressants inhibit nerve cells. If overused, more of the calcium channels that allow electrical charges to enter the nerve cells are created. With withdrawal both new and old cells are reactivated causing intense electrical charges to surge through the body. It is discovered that offspring of alcoholics lack the p3 typically missing in alcoholics, which means that this illness can be inherited. Many persons die from choking, freezing, drowning, automobile accidents due to lack of control, resulting from overuse of a depressant. Medical science warns pregnant women against disturbances in the development of the fetus caused by even minimal use of alcohol. Nor can activities such as gambling substitute for the exciting reward of realizing a full measure of creativity.

Recent experiments have shown what the orient had long ago discovered, that we have considerably more control over our senses than we exercise. Sensation of pain often can be controlled. Although animals and man alike experience pain as a warning signal of physical injury, the human being adds to his pain an intellectual interpretation of its cause. The *pain* is on the part of the senses, but the *hurt* is due to our habit of judging causes in terms of an ego/non-ego dichotomy. If the pain is interpreted to mean rejection by the non-ego, it will become acute. For example, if a person having his teeth fixed looks upon the dentist as the non-ego doing him an injustice, the pain will hurt him because he adds to it a feeling of injury.

The Melzack-Wall Spinal Gate Theory points out that our interpretation of pain can close the gate in the spinal column and prevent the transference of pain to the brain.

> Feelings such as anxiety, fear or sadness open it (the gate), allowing more pain messages to reach the brain, while positive feelings such as joy or exhilaration close it.[14]

If pain takes us by surprise the first onslaught will be felt with intensity but, on closing the gate in the spinal column, it will quickly subside. The body, in addition, has natural pain killers. Endorphine released by the pituitary gland can be 200 times as effective a pain suppressant as morphine. Other areas of our body that were formerly believed to be controlled by the autonomous nervous system are now perceived to be subject to mind control. By using biofeedback, blood pressure can be lowered, some kinds of headache alleviated, and other physical disorders corrected by concentrating our mind on the process and imagining it as it should take place. There have been many studies made of the effect of the mind upon the body with surprising results. For example, in multiple personalities, one personality may have a severe allergy which disappears immediately when another personality appears. An experiment with a control group of alcoholics, who were not allowed to take a drink for several days, resulted in their becoming inebriated when they were told they were being served hard liquor, when actually it was a soft drink served in a cocktail glass. On the other hand, alcoholics did not feel any effect from alcohol when it was disguised as a soft drink. The paraphernalia associated with the use of narcotics is as attractive to the user as the drug itself, which demonstrates that peer group values can be a strong influence.

The Relation of World and Body According to Contemporary Philosophy

Since contemporary philosophy, namely phenomenology and existentialism, has as its presupposition: the principles of lived experience reveal Dasein, the question posed concerning the senses will be: What can lived experience tell us about our material dimension? Lived experience contradicts the tendency of science to consider the human body as object; *my* body is not just *a* body. Dasein realizes its destiny in the space/time dimension through the medium of *my* body. Luijpen says

> *My* body, therefore, is not the body described by physiology or drawn by anatomy. The body which occurs in anatomy, biology, and physiology is merely *a* body. These sciences describe the body as a thing in the world. Their descriptions are based upon the observations by men of science, but they do not explicitate my perception of my body as mine.[15]

Marcel points out the difference between *my* body and external objects. An object is such that its presence entails a possible absence. The object of *having* has a certain exteriority and foreignness, existing independently of me. Unlike my body, I can within certain limits dispose of what I *have*.[16] But since it is tied up with my existence, I cannot dispose of my body.

For Merleau-Ponty, although the body is not itself an *object*, it is that which makes it possible to know objects. Objects cannot be understood except through my body, since it is the "the resistance of my body to all variation of perspective" that makes awareness of external objects possible.[17]

Luijpen illustrates this:

> My hand reveals itself as mine when I try to grasp an object; my feet manifest themselves as mine when I carefully place them on the steps of a steep staircase; my eyes disclose themselves as mine when I let my gaze travel over the world.[18]

It is my body which *catches* and *comprehends* movement. When we dance, play music, write, play baseball, we do not plan our movements but the corporeal body itself is *incorporated* into the goal of the action. Through it I am able to have a world. I touch a fruit and know its texture; I taste its sweetness and know its composition. For contemporary philosophy, lived experience replaces the method of science since science has depersonalized the human person by attempting to deprive us of all contact with objects, advising that taste, color, and so forth exist only in the brain.

> There was a time when scientific circles judged it very abnormal to assume that I really smell delicious apples and really see green grass. They preferred to start from physico-chemical stimuli or from physiologically described organs and thus no longer attained to perception.[19]

Since my body is never *a body*, it can never be known without consideration of the self which directs its acts. Since the relation of the self to the body is essentially irreversible, we cannot equate a human being to an object. To do so would degenerate the body into a *representation* of a body - a manikin, a robot, a machine. Perception is always by a self and its body is that in which *world* is revealed.

This is particularly true of personal sensations. For example, we can sense *through our body* whether or not we are welcomed by the other. The other's resistance is not immediately understood but felt. No objective account of the actions of the other could reveal what is communicated by his body. Language reveals this *bodily* communication in such expressions as *bristling, sneering, helpless, demurely, drooping, frowning*. On the other hand, words involving an intellectual appraisal are not generally verbs which express a bodily stance but are adverbs describing a mental state, such as: arrogantly, appeasingly, compatibly. Body language reveals an attitude toward us not revealed in speech. Luijpen notes that

> I encounter the other as the other, as a subject, when he looks at me with love, hatred, or indifference, when he throws me a gesture, when he assumes a threatening attitude, when he addresses me in speech, for his body is the embodiment of his subjectivity.[20]

To contemporary philosophy, having a body means accessibility. We can make ourselves accessible to the other by means of a friendly gesture even before we have an intellectual appreciation of him. Adults are very often afraid to smile, to become *as little children*, as Jesus recommends. Emotion is a natural means of communication and should not be disguised. Without feeling or emotion, we remain aloof, limiting our world rather than listening to the voice of Being as it speaks to us through the other.

The Development of the Senses According to Piaget

The unfolding of the understanding is dependent upon the increased capacity of the senses. *What particular development of the senses is necessary before the child is able to use his immaterial powers?* is the question raised by Jean Piaget. A necessary but not sufficient condition of the ability of the intellectual power to understand is a corresponding development of the sense power, e.g., before the concept of square feet can be understood, the child must overcome his fixation upon a single dimension. The power of understanding is closely associated with the overcoming of ego-centrism and an increased awareness of his surroundings before the child can begin to operate effectively in the Formal Period of adult life. Since the intellectual power uses the data of the senses, the child must learn to focus upon essential data in the environment. If he cannot organize the material of his senses, the child cannot take the further step of organizing intellectual data. Piaget

Our Sensist Dimension 55

maps out four periods of development which represent an expansion of consciousness.[21] Both language and number have their basis in reality and an increasing awareness of the external world as well as a keen awareness of the interplay of causes contribute to the child's ability to form his world-model.

Sensorimotor Period: 1 - 2 yrs.
    Object permanence to object flexibility
    One to one to many to one relationship
    Means only to means to end relation
    Ritual play to symbolic play

Pre-operational Period: 2 - 7 yrs.
    Concreteness
    Irreversibility
    Ego-centrism
    Centering
    States vs. transformations
    Transductive reasoning

Concrete Operations Period: 7-11 yrs.
    Expansion of consciousness
    Cardination and ordination
    Relating of part to whole
    Overcoming of ego-centrism

Formal Period: 11 yrs. on
    Use of immaterial powers to:
    Understand logic
    Distinguish contradictories
    Operate on an operation
    Figure volume

In the sensorimotor period, a necessary, though not sufficient condition for understanding motion, is the ability of the child to progress from object permanence to object flexibility, e.g., focusing upon a moving object.

Second, the ability to see an object from many perspectives is a necessary condition for the sharing of a common language. The child, for example, progresses from a one to one relationship, in which each object must have its own name, to many different names for the same object, and the reverse. Piaget's child, finding a shell, pretended to drink, calling it a *cup*, then placed it on her head, calling it a *hat*, and finally called it a *boat in the water*.[22] The ability to sense the relation between means and end is prerequisite to the ability of the intellectual power to set up a value system. At first the child merely imitates something without intending any purpose for it as when a child opens his mouth when his mother is eating her soup. In a means to end relation the child does not merely imitate the ball rolling under the sofa but uses his own means of going around the end table to fetch it.[23] The fourth characteristic is basic to learning a common language. The child progresses from ritual play to symbolical play. Whereas the former is merely imitative, the latter requires the child's self-initiated *pretend* play. This symbolic play is internalized to form the symbols of the child's private language, making it possible for him to later learn a common language.

In the Pre-Operational Period, although his world is still largely materialistic, the child begins to overcome his total dependence upon his senses. Nevertheless, all of the following characteristics must be overcome before the child can advance to the Formal stage of immaterial operation. Concreteness simply means the child is tied to his physical environment since he operates on sense level. Irreversibility is evident in that the child can add two numbers but cannot subtract, or when asked if he has a brother, although answering *Yes*, will, when asked if his brother has a brother, answer *No*. Egocentrism continues although the child is able to communicate with his playmates and learn to play games. Centering refers to the fact that the child is unable to focus upon more than one dimension. He believes that one of two equal balls of clay becomes greater when rolled out in the shape of a sausage because it now has more width. This *centering* makes it impossible for him to understand two or more dimensions as in square feet or volume. States vs. transformations refers to an inability to see illustration A as representing a stick in motion rather than five different sticks (see below).[24]

Transductive reasoning refers to the Humean type pseudo-causality typical of this period. In pseudo-causality the child believes, that since she wears her

Our Sensist Dimension

party dress for parties, by putting on the dress, a party will follow.

In the Concrete Operations Period the child increases his ability to expand his consciousness. Before this period his consciousness is limited in that he cannot relate objects within a sufficiently wide perspective to understand natural laws such as the law of gravity. He conceives the level of water in a glass to be permanently fixed even when laid on its side. In the concrete period, he perceives the water in relation to the wider perspective of the table or ground.[25]

a   b

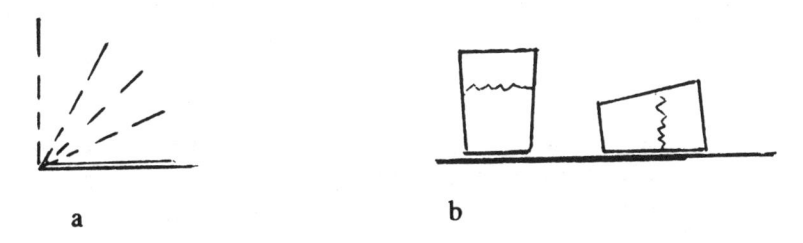

He also begins to see things from the other's point of view as in the following experiment.[26] He sits in front of the cones as illustrated in view (a) and is asked to draw what he would see if standing at one side (b) and behind the cones (c). This freedom from self-centeredness is essential for the immaterial power to be able to understand things from another's viewpoint.

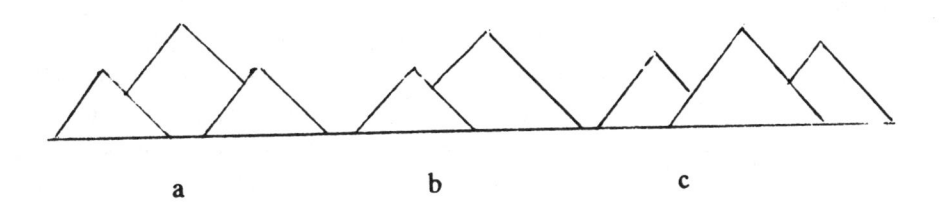

a   b   c

In the Concrete Period the child develops the ability to ordinate and cardinate members of a series - the forerunner of his ability to understand mathematics. During the Pre-operational period, if the child was given ten paper dolls of increasing size and ten corresponding canes so that "the dolls can go walking," he was unable to relate the canes to the size of the doll. Nor could he ordinate, demonstrated by his inability to reverse the order of the canes.[27] By the Concrete Operations period, however, he can not only reverse the order but can determine which one of the reversed canes belongs to which doll, an act requiring both cardination and ordination.

An important prelude to understanding logic is the ability developed in the Concrete Operations Period of relating part to whole. This inability occurring during the Pre-operational Period is demonstrated in the following experiment:

> The child is asked to count twenty wooden beads placed in a dish which he does correctly, indicating he understands the meaning of *wooden beads*. Eighteen brown beads are then placed in another dish, leaving two white beads remaining. He is then asked to count the brown beads which he also does correctly. However, when asked which will make the longer necklace, the wooden beads or the brown beads, he surprisingly answers the brown beads.[28]

The child could not see that brown and white beads equal wooden beads. By the time the child has reached the Concrete Operations Period he is able to understand a part to whole relation, but not until the Formal Period can he apply it to logic.

In the final period or Formal Operations, in which the immaterial power is now operating, the child can understand the form of a logical syllogism such as: All men are rational; Peter is a man; therefore Peter is rational. At this time, the child not only operates with sensible objects by organizing, testing, and observing them but can devise a scientific hypothesis by operating on this operation. He has learned to use his intellectual power without the necessity of manipulating materials. He can abstract from particular space and time, can distinguish contradictories such as the possible/impossible, and understand principles such as act and potency. In this formal period the intellectual power comes into its own, surpassing what is possible for the senses alone.

The important role of the senses in relating self to world should not be underestimated. We live in a space and time dimension and our immaterial knowledge derives its data and its analogies from occurrences that are material in nature. On the other hand, since our sense operation is controlled by the way we understand something, our sense images demonstrate the particular reference we give to them. We do not merely see, but with our immaterial power of will, we direct our senses to the various ends we have chosen. Our actions are not predetermined by what we sense, but what we sense is due to our own selectivity. James notes:

> Hence, even in the field of sensation, our minds exert a certain arbitrary choice. By our inclusions and omissions we trace the field's extent; by our emphasis we mark its foreground and its background; by our order we read it in this direction or in that. We receive in short the block of marble, but we carve the statue ourselves.[29]

Either to claim that knowledge consists solely of sensations as in materialism or, on the other hand, to consider sense knowledge to be nothing more than mere opinion as in Platonism, denigrates the important role of our senses in aiding our understanding to come to terms with a real world.

Summary

Materialism:

Presupposition: Only sense knowledge has validity.

Question: Do the senses conform to a real world?

Conclusion: Since the senses cannot observe a necessary connection, they do not know if there is or is not a real world.

Immaterialism:

Presupposition: Our sense images are given to us directly by God.

Question: Can sense images, which are material, be known by a mind which is immaterial?

Conclusion: The theory is contradictory.

Traditional:

Presupposition: Man possesses both sense and intellectual powers.

Question: Can we know extra-mental reality?

Conclusion: Intellectual power perceives a necessary connection between the sense image and the extra-mental reality.

Contemporary:

Presupposition: By lived experience we perceive the manifestation of Being.

Question: Is reality perceived by sense or intellectual power?

Conclusion: The self directs the senses to perceive the real world in the light of its understanding.

1. David Hume, *An Enquiry Concerning Human Understanding* from *The Essential Works*, ed. R. Cohen (New York: Bantam Books, 1965), p. 51

2. Ibid., p. 158. Author's parenthesis

3. Ibid., p. 78

4. Ibid., p.54. Animals also have imagination, demonstrated by their R.E.M. (rapid eye movements in dreaming)

5. Ibid., p. 57

6. Berkeley, *Principles of Human Knowledge*, II, 61

7. Ibid

8. William James, *Psychology* (New York: Collier Books, 1962), p. 254

9. Rudolf Arnheim, *Visual Thinking* (Berkeley: University of California Press, 1969), pp. 108-09

10. Ibid., p. 107

11. Ibid., p. 108

12. Roy B. Pinchot, ed. "The Brain," *The Human Body* (Washington, D.C.: U.S. News Books, 1981), p. 32

13. Ibid.

14. Helen Neal, "The Spinal Gate Theory of Pain," *American Pharmacy*, Vol. N.S. 18 #12 (Nov., 1978), p. 11

15. William A. Luijpen, *Existential Phenomenology* (Pittsburgh: Duquesne University Press, 1965), p. 187

16. Gabriel Marcel, *Being and Having*, trans. K. Farrer (New York: Harper & Row, 1965), pp. 154- 174

17. Maurice Merleau-Ponty, *Phenomenology of Perception* (London: Routledge & Kegan Paul, 1965), p. 92

18. Luijpen, *Existential Phenomenology*, p. 187

19. Ibid., p. 181

20. Ibid. pp. 188-189

21. John L. Phillips, Jr. *The Origins of Intellect, Piaget's Theory* (San Francisco: W. H. Freeman & Co., 1969), p. 59

22. Jean Piaget, *Play, Dreams, and Imitation in Childhood*, trans. C. Gattegno and F. M. Hodgson (New York: W. W. Norton, 1951), p. 124

23. Jean Piaget, *The Construction of Reality in the Child*, trans. M. Cook (New York: Basic Books, 1954), p. 205

24. Ibid., p. 64

25. Ibid., p. 86

26. Ibid., p. 84

27. Ibid., pp. 81-83

28. Jean Piaget, *The Child's Conception of Number* (New York: W. W. Norton, l965), p. 165. Reprinted by permission of Humanities Press, Atlantic Highlands, N.J. 07716

29. William James, *Pragmatism* from *The Works of William James* (Cambridge: Harvard University Press, 1975), p. 119

Chapter III

THE DIMENSION OF UNDERSTANDING

Since the human person's uniqueness resides in his immaterial powers, we turn now to the dimension of understanding. How does understanding differ from sensation? This question has been raised by many philosophers and remains a controversial question. The answer is dependent upon the idea of being expressed by each.

The Falsity of the Understanding According to Materialism

We would look in vain for an explanation of intellectual understanding in materialism since, for Hume, only sense experience is reliable. It is better, he said, to rely on mechanism or instinct since it is not probable that anything so essential to the subsistence of all human creatures

> could be trusted to the fallacious deductions of our reason, which is slow in its operations; appears not, in any degree, during the first years of infancy; and at best is, in every age and period of human life, extremely liable to error and mistake. It is more conformable to the ordinary wisdom of nature to secure so necessary an act of the mind, by some instinct or mechanical tendency, which may be infallible in its operations, may discover itself at the first appearance of life and thought, and may be independent of all the labored deductions of the understanding.[1]

Hume is adamant in his rejection of immaterial knowledge. Although he accepts sensations as valid, all other knowledge except quantity and number is excluded as erroneous. When we look over a library, he says, we should ask the question:

Does it contain any experimental reasoning (i.e., sense knowledge) concerning matters of fact and existence? No. Commit it then to the flames: For it can contain nothing but sophistry and illusion.[2]

Although Hume is correct in that our senses are vital to operating in the time and space dimension, he denigrates our immaterial power of intellect by which we can understand being. For the materialist, being indicates nothing more than a particular time and space. To say, *It is*, means, *It is here* rather than *there*. To reduce being to nothing more than *being here* is due to materialism's refusal to admit any knowledge other than sensation. *It is*, as contradictory to *It is not* cannot be known in an image. Consequently, existence for the materialist is reduced to the spatial. As Aristotle points out, this locative notion of being is the way of the common man. The sister in the following cartoon illustrates how the materialist understands being.

The Dimension of Understanding
According to Immaterialism

The immaterialist agrees with traditional philosophy, i.e., our mind is immaterial and is capable of intellectual understanding. How then does his notion of understanding differ from that of traditional philosophy? For Berkeley, sensations are given to us by God and it is these clearly perceived sense images which we call reality. If our thoughts agree with the "reality" that is put in our mind by God, then we have truth. However, we may find that oftentimes our sensations are misleading, and, rather than conforming to the sense image, we correct the sensation with our intellectual power. In the search for real causes to explain data, we constantly check sensations against the reasoning of our intellectual power. It appears, for example, that the sun is moving across the sky while we are remaining stationary, whereas we know intellectually that it is the earth moving on its axis which makes the sun appear to move. In such a case, could it be said that truth consists in conformity of intellect to sense image? Or do we, with our intellectual power, overrule the sensation in order to attain truth? If our sense impressions are given to us by God, as Berkeley contends, to judge them to be in error would appear to make the human person more of an authority on truth than Berkeley's God. For Berkeley, immaterial abstractions, which he calls *useless and impracticable*[3] are not real nor true and, therefore, could not improve upon sensation. Skepticism in regard to intellectual knowledge turns immaterialism into its opposite, i.e., materialism.

Since Berkeley claims to be an immaterialist, it would seem more logical for him to have credited truth to the immaterial mind. Plato, who, in this respect, leans toward immaterialism, does just that. For Plato, intellectual knowledge consists in a priori intuition of forms. These forms, known first hand in a prior life, are perceived in this life through reminiscence. If we understand, for example, two things to be equal, it is because we knew, in a heaven prior to living this life, the universal *equality*, the true form of which the *equality* in this world is merely a copy. Sensations are appearances rather than real. In other words, truth resides in the universal form known a priori. The presupposition on which Plato ordered his philosophy can be stated: Universal forms are true whereas sensations are mere appearances. It is not, as for Berkeley, sensations that must be accepted unconditionally but the intellect's universal forms. And since the sensible world does not possess the perfection of the absolute forms, knowledge of this world, rather than being true, consists merely of appearances. But, for a finite mind, is truth to be found in another realm, as Plato contends, or in the knowledge we have of our present world? Plato himself saw this problem and in his later writings looked beyond his theory of forms to account for the intellect's ability to distinguish truth from falsity.

For immaterialism, truth is not measured and tested against a real world but rather consists in the perfectionist ideals set up by the mind. In so doing the human person becomes confused over the possible vs. the impossible. Since, with his intellectual powers he can imagine more than is possible to realize in a world limited by time and space, he often becomes a perfectionist. This leads to frustration. In order that we may choose realistically between alternatives, it is essential to make a careful distinction between what is and what is not possible in a real world. Whereas the error committed by materialism is that it negates that which is and so commits reductionism, the error of immaterialism is that it affirms that which is not and so constructs an ideal rather than a real world.

The Dimension of Understanding According to Traditional Philosophy

For traditional philosophy, all judgments are grounded in the notion of being. Because we know that being is and is not not, we can affirm the existence of all other things. If being is, then the existence of John, as a being, can be affirmed. If being were not, the existence of John as a being would be contradictory. However the statement, *Being is not*, is unintelligible. Since being, by its very meaning, is the existent, it cannot be said to be non-existent. Therefore, it is being that establishes the parameters of intellectual power. Although some philosophers deny that the word *being* has any meaning, there is hardly a word spoken in the English language that does not either pose a question about the *to be* of beings or answer it with an affirmation or a negation of being. All sentences that employ the verb *to be* in one of its forms of past, present, or future are judgments of existence. Contractions sometimes disguise the reference to being. For example, the statement, *Mike swims*, is merely a contraction of the meaning, *Mike is* (rather than is not) and *is* (rather than is not) *swimming*.

Whether expressed by the language or not, the reality of being is evident to all who operate with their immaterial powers. We constantly affirm or negate as we compare our intellectual word with our sensations of reality. And though we may err at times, it is only by means of our understanding in correspondence with reality that we can know truth. Neither sense nor intellectual knowledge is infallible. Sensations are neither true nor false in themselves nor are immaterial abstractions or universals. But truth comes to be in the existential judgment which is an adequation between reality and thought. We attain truth when, with our intellectual power, we affirm that which is and negate that which is not.

The presupposition for traditional philosophy is that, through reason, we can know reality objectively which not only encompasses all that is known of the time and space dimension but includes man's relation to infinite Being. By affirming that which is and negating that which is not, we have the knowledge needed to live realistically and with justice. However, since our intellectual power is under our direction, we can also misuse it. By negating that which is we can deny the humanity of a person, a sect, or a race of people and by such a denial no longer require ourselves to observe their rights, e.g., slavery. If we are oblivious to possible being, the error of materialism, we will be pessimistic, giving up hope and thus failing to fulfill our destiny. If, on the other hand, we mistakenly affirm that which is not, the error of immaterialism, we are in danger of living a Pollyanna existence, always expecting the impossible. Correspondence of our affirmations with *that which is* and our negations with *that which is not* provides us with a true appraisal of our world.

No amount of development of a sense power could make it capable of operating intellectually, i.e., immaterially, just as we cannot, by adding to an extended object, transform it into an object without dimension. Since with our intellectual power we affirm or negate being, which is an entirely different operation from the image-making power of the senses, the two powers are radically different in kind. The biologist Goldstein says:

> Even in its simplest form (immaterial) abstraction is separate in principle from concrete behavior. There is no gradual transition from the one to the other. The assumption of an attitude toward the abstract is not more complex merely through the addition of a new factor of determination; it is a totally different activity of the organism.[4]

Why does it require a power that is immaterial to affirm or to negate the existence of beings? We can affirm being only because we can negate being. This requires an immaterial power because non-being has no physical dimension and therefore exceeds the capacity of the material sense powers. And since the senses cannot know non-being, they also cannot know being. To understand opposites we must be able to differentiate them. If they are indistinguishable, they are unintelligible. For example, if everything had always been the same temperature, would we know what cold or hot is? Because of our unique power of negation, we can contrast the contradictories, being and non-being, and thus understand being. Non-being might be compared to the zero which is needed in order to understand arithmetic although it represents no quantity of its own.

Every statement we make either states implicitly or implies an affirmation or negation of being. Although the senses cannot have an image of being nor of not being, both possibilities must be present to the intellectual power in order that a choice can be made between them, (otherwise we would be able to agree with each contradictory as it is presented). We then adhere to one side of the contradictory. The affirmation *Yes*, added to the statement *Craig is*, does not add new meaning but implies a choice has been made in the affirmative *Yes, Craig is* or in the negative *No, Craig is not*. This is a self-reflective process, demonstrating that we are aware of our own act of affirming or negating.

We are able to affirm or negate the existence of something because, by means of our intellectual power, we can self-reflect. Since the power of intellect is not limited by time and space, we are present to ourselves as the one knowing and the thing known. We are conscious of telling a lie because we are aware of ourselves in the act of constructing a false proposition in which we affirm existence of the non-existent or vice versa. Whereas the senses are aware of only one image at a time, there are three truths present simultaneously to our intellectual power: our knowledge, the act of distorting that knowledge, and the false statement.

The intellectual power, unlike sense power, cannot make an image. It understands by relating knowledge to being. Being as such does not designate any particular being and therefore is not limited to the material conditions of the particular. Since it is not limited to a particular time and space, the intellectual power can understand contraries simultaneously whereas the sense powers can know only one contrary at a time, e.g., if I am receiving a stimulus of heat from a stove, I am not able, at the same time, to perceive it as cold. With intellectual power we can understand contraries simultaneously as relative to each other, e.g., forty degrees is hot compared to 10 degrees but cold compared to 70 degrees.

The self-reflective process is not merely a turning back after the event to compare, but a simultaneous double or triple action not possible to sense powers, limited by the fact that two material things cannot occupy the same time and space. By self-reflection we are also aware of the double action of knowing we know something or knowing we don't know it.

With our immaterial power we also reflect upon our senses. Kant points out that the apperceptions of our intellect add to our knowledge by organizing sense data into a coherent whole. By reflecting upon our senses we can examine their data in the light of our understanding of causality and other first principles and judge whether or not they are valid. When driving a car on a hot day, if we see what appears to be a pool of shimmering water above the pavement, we judge it to be light waves caused by heat. Contrary to Hume and Berkeley, we distinguish dream from reality on a more substantial basis than that of clear/unclear.

How do we compose an intellectual word? Although our sense images are ready-made, since our intellectual power is self-reflective, we are aware of our own acts and know how we compose a sentence or other meaning unit (called a word in philosophy). We join a predicate to a subject, grammatically speaking, or join accidental properties to a subject or substance, philosophically speaking. For example, in the sentence *The tree is green*, the accidental property *green* is joined to the substance *tree*. The word *is* serves as a copula joining substance and accident.

The use of the copula *is* is common to both sense and intellectual powers. What, then, is the difference between an animal's language, viz., the stringing together of labels, and human language? For the senses, the word *is* is merely a device to join one image to another, e.g., apple and red. On the other hand, for our intellectual power the word *is* not only acts as a copula but has meaning for us as an affirmation of the being of that which we are thinking about, e.g., *The apple is* (rather than *is not*) and *is* (rather than *is not*) *red*. Although the sentence draws attention to the color of the apple, there is also implied a reference to its extra-mental existence. Sometimes the inflection with which we speak the word *is* draws attention to the existential factor, i.e., greater emphasis distinguishes real existence from a hypothetical construct, e.g., Cinderella *is* a girl (not just a character).

In order that being be made manifest, it must be transformed into the understood; it must be rendered meaningful. The intellectual word shares the same principles as the existent but in a different mode. As defined by Thomas Aquinas, the traditional notion of truth is a commensuration between our intellect and extramental reality.[5] This is more clearly perceived if we observe what St. Augustine says about reality: God created beings by giving them species, mode, and order.[6] We know their species in a word of definition. We affirm the mode or the being of beings in a word of existential judgment. And when we evaluate the good possessed by the existent we know its measure. To know the mode, species, and measure (perfection) of a thing is to know its reality and its truth. These three moments of the intellectual procession of words are commensurate to the extra-mental reality. The *verbum* of definition, in focusing upon the universal aspects of the existent, abstracts from its materiality and specifies it according to what it has in common with other beings. The *verbum* of existential judgment, or second moment, is intentionally proportionate to the being of the existent as an individual, insofar as the individual is differentiated from others of the same species. In most instances, the self must reflect upon the senses, applying universal characteristics to the sense image. In the third moment, or word of the heart, there is complete manifestation of the reality in its fullness of being, i.e., as a good. Whereas with our senses we are not aware of being; with our intellectual power we are able to attain to the truth of being.

But how can we know that when we affirm something that it really is and when we negate something that it really is not? Aquinas says that we not only know through our sense report and immaterial abstractions but we understand first principles of being with which we compare our judgments, e.g., every effect has a cause. Since first principles have their basis in reality, to ignore a first principle is to ignore reality. If we believe something in contradiction to a first principle, it is our judgment that is at fault.

In summary, some of the differences between the operation of our intellectual power and our sense power are:

Differences in Operation of Sense and Intellectual Power

Sense Power	Intellectual Power
1. cannot have an image and not have an image of something.	1. can know being and non-being simultaneously.
2. matches or mismatches an object or an action with its name.	2. knows truth and falsity.
3. knows only one contrary at a time, e.g., either hot or cold.	3. knows contraries simultaneously, e.g. 60 degrees is hot compared to 30 degrees but cold compared to 90 degrees.
4. cannot self-reflect, e.g., eye cannot see itself seeing.	4. can self-reflect, e.g. we know that we know or know that we don't know.
5. can do only one operation at a time.	5. can do two or more operations simultaneously, e.g., knowing the truth, the false, and that you are telling a lie.
6. are not conscious of how the image is produced.	6. is conscious of how a sentence is constructed, e.g., we place subject before verb, etc.

Comparisons Between Sense and Immaterial Ways of Knowing

There are a number of questions related to being that we are constantly asking which point up the meaning that being has for us. They provide a framework in which the human person can understand his world and transcend beyond it. The most basic of questions is *Is it?* Since this question can only be answered by posing *being* against its contradictory *non-being*, it extends the power of intellect to its maximum capacity. Although it is the simplest of questions, if we could not answer this question, we could neither ask nor answer any other questions about being. Since all other questions are meaningless unless there is being, the most basic question, *Is it?* is implied in all other questions, e.g., What *is it?*; Why *is it?*

The question, *Is it?* can only be asked or answered by a power that affirms or negates being. Those who adhere to materialism will object at this point that the word *is* has no reference to existence but merely serves as a statement of the presence or absence of a being. For example, since materialism reduces the meaning of being to indicate merely a locality in time and space: the question, *Is it?* means *Is it here?* But presence is not all that is indicated by the statement, *You are*. Rather it means that you *are* rather than *are not*. You may not be *here*, but you, nevertheless, *are*. Our being is more comprehensive than our physical place.

Since the question, *Is it?* refers to the *esse* or existence of beings, it is always answered by yes or no regardless of the kind of being considered. *Esse* allows of no differentiation; whether a stone or a man the answer is Yes, it (he) is or No, it (he) is not.

The differentiation of being belongs to the second question, *What is it?* This question refers to the essence or limitation of being. As previously stated, finite beings are composed of a principle of *esse* which makes them to be and of essence which limits them to be a particular kind of being. *Esse* tells us *that* the being is; essence tells us *what* or *who* the being is. Because each thing is limited to a different degree, we are able to differentiate beings according to their natures (essences). In all sentence constructions in the English language we refer both to the *esse* of something and its essence. In the sentence, *The apple is red*, the word *is* affirms the *esse* or existence of the apple answering the question, *Is it?* and the word *apple* names the essence of the object answering the question, *What is it?* Although not all languages so conveniently point out the relation between *esse* and essence, nevertheless, since these principles are based on reality, they are true whether or not they are expressed by the language.

Since a materialist accepts only sensations as valid, in asking the question, *What is it,* he refers only to physical entities, merely inquiring after the name of the object. For the chimpanzee Lana, for example, the question means, *What name-of-this?* The classification of beings then takes place by material generalization (induction) following Hume's principles of resemblance, contiguity, and (pseudo) causality. Goldstein reports that his aphasiac patient, when asked to name animals, replied: "a polar bear, a brown bear, a lion, a tiger." However, that she did not know these animals by their essence but merely according to the time and space they occupied, is clear from her explanation: "If we enter the zoological gardens, we come at first to the polar bear and then to the other animals." Goldstein explains that,"rather than knowing the animals by their essence, she had obviously recalled the animals as they were situated in the zoological gardens and had used the words only as belonging to the concrete situation."[7] The induction engaged in by the senses is too embedded in the concrete situation to be able to arrive at the knowledge of essences. Just as the perimeters of an object cannot be sensed unless we have an image of the object, the limit (essence) of a being cannot be known unless it is known *to be*. And since the senses cannot affirm its being, they cannot know the limit of its being. The question, *What is it?*, for the senses is merely asking for the name of the object.

When we answer the question, *What is it?* with our immaterial powers, we abstract the essence immaterially. This does not remove the object from the extra-mental world but considers its characteristic traits within the concrete situation. Aquinas states that it is because these traits transcend the particular instance of it that the resulting abstraction is immaterial. That which is essential to the object is considered from the standpoint of its causality, either as a cause or as caused. This is a rational explanation of the interdependence and interaction of one being with another, essential to its constitution.

There are many other questions that follow upon knowledge of the *esse* or being of the existent, such as What *is* it?, How *is* it?, When *is* it?, and Where *is* it? These questions do not refer merely to the material dimension of the object. Each question pertains to being and so includes within itself some form of the verb *to be* whether implied implicitly or directly. Let us first consider the question, Why is it? This question is answered *because*, referring to the being of the cause. Why is Sean the cause of this painting? Because he has given it *esse*, making it to be when otherwise it would not have been. In addition, he has given it essence, making it to be this painting rather than something else. Since the senses can know neither *esse* nor essence, we must use our intellectual powers to know whether or not a cause has sufficient being to create a particular effect.

The question, How is it? is answered by the senses merely by manipulating physical objects to get the desired effect - by trial or error, by imitation, or by imagining the rearrangement of physical objects. When we ask the question with our intellectual power, however, we are making an inquiry into the relation of one nature or essence with another. This requires consideration of the constancy of the particular kind of interaction, giving rise to scientific law. In inquiring how electricity works, the senses merely want to know how this plug fits into the socket. To answer the question immaterially is to know how a positive charge or proton acts with a negative charge or electron, providing the understanding that is necessary to originate a novel electrical layout without actually manipulating materials. Only an immaterial power can know essences or natures; therefore it is only with our intellectual power that we are able to know the relation of one essence to another to answer the question, How is it?

The senses can answer the question, Where is it? only by reference to the physical place where the person is at the time. For example, Goldstein tells about an aphasiac patient who could take an elevator to another floor and without difficulty find the ward where she was to work. However, when led into the wrong corridor she was unable to find her way back to the ward or even to the elevator.[8] Since the senses are immersed in the concrete situation, the patient could not detach herself from her surroundings in order to perceive herself in relation to other possible locations. For the immaterial intellect, the questions of when and where are answered by a series in which

The Dimension of Understanding

the more immediate is encompassed by a far wider perspective beyond the reach of the senses. The room I am in is in a building which is located in a state, country, continent, hemisphere, world, galaxy, universe, and so forth. It is also impossible for the senses to perceive this series if it is a political division rather than merely a spatial division, e.g., Alaska and Hawaii are part of the United States although not contiguous to the mainland. Since our immaterial power is not immersed in the material dimension, we can abstract ourselves from our situation and see ourselves from different vantage points such as in reading a map or a diagram. Goldstein notes that abstract behavior is brought into play whenever the ego must be detached from the situation.

That the question, When is it? cannot be grasped by the senses in any meaningful way is illustrated by an aphasiac patient. Although he always arrived for his appointment on time, his knowledge was determined by the physical location of the hands of the clock. When both hands of the clock pointed to three he left home. Since it took forty-five minutes to take the bus, he arrived at four o'clock. However, he was unable to say where the hands of the clock would be at a specific time since time units had no meaning for him.[9] With our immaterial power, however, we understand time through a series consisting of the number of seconds in a minute, of minutes in an hour, and so forth, requiring an understanding of the relation of one unit to another. The immaterial intellect can understand the basis for these units, e.g., that a day is based upon the turning of the earth on its axis in relation to the sun and so on.

Aristotle's definition of time as the measure of motion across space in respect to a before and after refers only to objective time. However, it is observed by contemporary philosophers that primordial time and place is more comprehensive and basic than objective time and place. We refer, for example, to our *longest hour* or to the swift passage of time, or *where* we are at this time of our life, our *distance* from our goals, and so forth. Bergson points out that spatialized time does not have the same meaning for the self as the inner time of real duration. Inner time is not broken up into units but, since the self is continually coming-to-be, is like a rolling snowball. As opposed to objective time which is measured and counted, duration is an inner experience which moves along under its own impetus in the "rhythmic organization of the whole."[10] It is known by intuition. For Heidegger, since we are beings who are coming-to-be, historicity belongs to us primordially. Because of this, we measure the spatialized time of the world rather than the reverse. Our understanding of the objective *where* and *when* stems from the more primordial question of what time and space mean to us as human beings.

The question, Can it be? for the senses is answered by actual trial and error. The animal discovers, by fighting, whether or not it is possible to win. On the other hand, Can it be? for the immaterial power refers to the difference between the possible versus the impossible, the latter being determined by whether or not the action is contradictory. We may propose a task which is difficult but not one that entails a contradiction, e.g., using up your time and yet having the same time unused.

The question Should it be? for the senses is decided on the basis of reward or punishment. The answer to the question proposed to the immaterial power, however, entails a sliding rule from good to evil or justice to injustice with every choice on the scale possible, making it a very discriminate choice. For example, if the scale is from one to ten, then four is a better choice of action than three but not as good as five, and so forth.

For traditional philosophy, just as with science, truth is considered to be the work of reason. Heidegger, however, contends that if traditional philosophy first defines philosophy as the pursuit of truth by reason and then proves its tenets to be valid because they are rational, its argument is circular. Since the opposite of the rational is the irrational, the latter is consequently held to be invalid. An example of this are the proofs for the existence of God known rationally as the absolute, omnipresent, omniscient act of pure *esse*. Although as speculative knowledge of God, this statement has validity, since all rational knowledge is itself indifferent, it seems to create an unbridgeable hiatus between man and God. What is missing, according to contemporary philosophy, is that the personal is not developed in its own right. Since contemporary philosophy seeks an understanding of *Dasein* through lived experience, it takes a holistic approach. It is by reflecting upon the interaction of all of our powers that we discover the mode of being of *Dasein*. Willpower is selective of the content of what is understood and emotion and mood add intensity to understanding. Intuitive processes often overlooked by traditional philosophy are the basis of creativity. The over-emphasis upon the rational has impoverished *Dasein* of the rich resources at its command.

What Is Thinking?
According to Contemporary Philosophy

For Heidegger, since Being is revealed to us through mood, feeling, and emotion, it makes little sense to limit the method of philosophy to rational analysis. If we enter into philosophy it will "concern us personally, affect us, and indeed, touch us in our very nature." Since its presupposition is lived experience rather than objective knowledge, contemporary philosophy believes we must be written into the notion of truth. We cannot expect to find an *objective truth* which will be the same for everyone. Rather we focus upon reality in a particular way and thus form our own world-model. Truth is not merely the product of our intellectual power but is determined to a large extent by will power with which we focus our attention. James asserts it is "the faculty of voluntarily bringing back a wandering attention over and over again" that "is the root of judgment, character, and will." He notes that learning is dependent upon the amount of interest that we have in a subject. Curiosity should be awakened so that in seeking answers to questions we knit new information onto our present understanding. James says:

> What we say about reality thus depends on the perspective into which we throw it. The *that* of it is its own; but the *what* depends on the *which* and the which depends on *us*.[11]

There is also a margin of error in knowing any truth due to our inability to fully comprehend Being. And since our way of being is a coming-to-be, truth will come-to-be for us as the possibilities of our being are actualized. A lack of Being is a lack of truth.

The objective certitude the skeptics look for can never be acquired by a being situated in-the-world. We must be aware of our involvement in the framing of our world in order to realize that it is possible for each to frame his or her world-model in a different way. This does not indicate that truth is relative but does take into account that a finite mind is not omniscient. The so-called objective truth of traditional philosophy has in too many instances in the past been considered to be absolute. To lay claim to an unchanging truth that we can *possess* is to ascribe to the human person superhuman powers. We cannot know truth with such exactitude, says contemporary philosophy. While not denying truth as a commensuration between mind and reality, it emphasizes our part in forming our world model.

Contemporary philosophy attempts to reconcile the subject/object dichotomy by including our role in the framing of our world and, at the same time, by preserving the role of Being itself as that which manifests itself to us. For example, because of the primordial way in which we have our being-in-the-world, the present-at-hand of nature does not oppose us as object to subject but "is grounded in *something we have in advance* - in a fore-having."[12] Our understanding, rather than merely abstracting, defining, and isolating reality objectively, perceives that the present-at-hand has a particular connotation of involvement with the self. We know the ready-at-hand or equipment, for example, not mainly by defining it, but in a fore-conception which is made explicit through the prepositional form of *as*, e.g., we know this box *as* a place for tools, *as* a stool to sit on, *as* a doll house, *as* a coffin, *as* firewood, *as* garbage, depending on our lived experience. The *as* aspect of the understanding not only precedes definition but reinstates the individuality of the object which is lost during abstraction. It is only in relation to world that the ready-to-hand has meaning and therefore an abstraction in itself is a lifeless concept that falls outside of world. For complete understanding a coincidence of the opposites of individual and universal is needed. Either to lose the individual through abstraction or to fail to see the universal in the individual is a form of anomalous behavior, according to Goldstein, who notes that our way of being oscillates between the abstract and the concrete.

> Normal behavior is characterized by an alternation between an attitude involving abstract and one involving concrete behavior, and this alternation is appropriate to the situation and the individuality, to the task for which the organism is set. If either attitude becomes independent and governs the behavior of a normal person too completely, then we are faced with an anomalous form of behavior.[13]

How do we frame our world and yet let Being be as it is? It is from out of Being that we come-to-be, says Heidegger. He equates the word Being with the Greek word *Logos* which is the gathering together of all beings.[14] Logos gathers all together in thought. But Being is covered over and hidden, and yet it is only in *Aletheia* or uncoveredness that Being can make itself known to us. We must make a clearing in order that we can hear the silent voice of Being. Heidegger astutely points out that, unfortunately, the most thought-provoking of thoughts in this thought-provoking time is that we are still not thinking.[15] What is thinking, then, that we are not engaging in it? If thinking and Being are the same, then, inasmuch as we fail to be concerned with Being, we are not thinking.

Rather than thinking we spend our time in idle talk. Idle talk and wayward curiosity distract us from the manifestation of Being. Heidegger notes that "by its very nature, idle talk is a closing-off since to go back to the ground of what is talked about is something which it leaves undone."[16] Our culture demonstrates that we are moved by the gigantic which overwhelms us, by the violent which stupifies us, and by the outrageous which excites us. Rather than seeking culture, we search for the novel at the expense of creativity. "Curiosity is everywhere and nowhere."[17] In inauthenticity we stand in subjection to the *they* of publicness. The *they* is *das Mann*, not any particular persons but people in general, who make up the world of everydayness or who comprise our clique. We are slaves to the voguish. The *they* tell us how we should comport ourselves, what we should wear, what we must believe, chooses the persons we are to admire. We uncritically accept their prejudices as justified, e.g., old age is ridiculous or senile. If someone acts out of character with publicness, we join forces in ostracizing him rather than commending him on his independent thinking.

Often television or other media set the moral tone of the *they*. What is advertised is accepted as valid just by becoming well known. This captivating of our judgment is often furthered by the atmosphere generated by the media, such as an aura of distrust of government, an excitement over war, an enticement with sex, or a morbid curiosity over criminal acts. We do not do our own thinking, but, rather, we become an *it* whose existence is to be used by others. "It itself *is* not; its Being has been taken away by the Others," says Heidegger.[18] In this inauthentic way of being, characterized by busyness and excitement, we *fall* into a world. Heidegger notes that the alienation of falling leads by its own movement to *Dasein's* getting entangled in itself. It is in fleeing its ownmost potentiality for being that *Dasein* gets entangled.

> This *absorption in...* has mostly the character of *Being lost* in the publicness of the *they*. Dasein has ... fallen away from itself as an authentic potentiality for Being its Self, and has fallen into the *world.*[19]

This self-entangling is at once tempting and tranquilizing. Dasein's plunge into the nullity of inauthentic everydayness remains hidden from Dasein "so much so, indeed, that it gets interpreted as a way of ascending and living concretely."[20] If we wish to live authentically, we must appropriate thought rather than follow what has been passed on to us by the *they*, says Heidegger. In order to fulfill our possibilities, we must overcome our desire to live peacefully with the *they* since the *they* is opposed to innovation, insisting on the status quo. Rather than losing ourselves in idle talk, we can first begin to think by learning to listen to the silent voice of Being. "What appeals to us as the voice of Being," says Heidegger, "evokes our correspondence."[21] It evokes the wonder we feel when we begin to realize that Being is as it is and not otherwise. We step back from Being in astonishment and yet "at the same time are forcibly drawn to and, as it were, held fast by that from which it (astonishment) retreats."[22] The mystery that is Being touches us to the quick, and, because we cannot grasp its meaning at once, we are overcome by a sense of the uncanny.

> Man is the strangest of all things... because he steps out, marches beyond his ordinary, customary, familiar boundaries, because, as active-power, he goes beyond the limit of the familiar, precisely in the direction of the uncanny in the sense of the overwhelming.[23]

Only insofar as we become "attuned" to the mystery that is Being, can we experience our as yet unrealized spiritual dimensions. This state of mind is primordial to any act of will that we might take to change the world and, in

# The Dimension of Understanding

fact, is the pre-condition of recognizing that the world should be changed.

We all have a part to play in thinking in order to bring a new world into being. Although we may not see its immediate effects, Heidegger notes that, clumsy and groping though it may be,

> sharing in thinking proves to be an unobtrusive sowing - a sowing that cannot be authenticated through the prestige or utility attaching to it - by sowers who may perhaps never see blade and fruit and may never know a harvest. They serve the sowing and even before that they serve its preparation.[24]

And even though we, ourselves, do not see the fruit of our thinking, we will, by taking thought, add to the composite of creative thinking which will hopefully bring about peace in the world. At the very least, we will come to realize the meaning that Being itself holds for us. Bragdon asserts that "never was truer word spoken than *seek and ye shall find* because that which is sought is itself the seeker."[25]

Summary

According to traditional philosophy, the operation of the immaterial intellectual power differs radically from sense operation. Since it is self-reflective, it is capable of two simultaneous operations. We not only know being but simultaneously self-reflect upon our intellectual operation to affirm the judgment: Yes, it is, or to negate it: No, it is not. Being is called self-evident since it is contradictory to contend that being is not and non-being is. Being circumscribes the parameters of intellectual power. There are no judgments that do not imply a reference to being. The immaterial power is uniquely human since questions answered by a higher animal, such as a chimpanzee, merely point to a particular spatial reality.

The following questions can be answered in two different ways as follows, depending upon whether they refer to sensations or immaterial understanding:

The question, Is it? is answered by

> Senses - It is *here* or it is *there*.
> Immaterial powers - It *is* rather than it *is not*

The question, What is it? is answered by

> Senses - The name of the object
> Immaterial powers - The essence (immaterial form, species or word of definition)

The question, Why is it? is answered by

> Senses - Pseudo-causality
> Immaterial powers - Real causality

The question, When is it? refers to

> Senses - the position of the hands of a clock
> Immaterial powers - motion of universe or internal time

The question, Where is it? is answered by

> Senses - the physical place surrounding the ego
> Immaterial powers - the political division of a state, abstraction of self on a map, or relation of parts of the universe.

The question, Should it be? is determined by

> Senses - reward and punishment
> Immaterial powers - a sliding rule from justice to injustice or from good to evil

The Dimension of Understanding

The question, Can it be? is determined by

> Senses - manipulating material objects or actions
> Immaterial powers - the contradictories, possible/impossible

Truth is defined by traditional philosophy as an adequation of the intellect's word or judgment to the extra-mental reality. It is necessary, not only to check the sense report but to refer the content to first principles of being. The judgment is correct if we affirm that which is and negate that which is not.

According to contemporary philosophy, mood and emotion, as well as understanding, reveal world and make us aware of 'how one is' and 'how one is faring', e.g., boredom indicates that one has formed his world with too few possibilities whereas frustration indicates the opposite. Truth is neither relative nor merely objective. We frame our own world, yet we let being be. To live authentically we need to go back to the ground of what is talked about in order to think for ourselves. However, we are still living in inauthenticity, lost in idle talk and subject to the *they* which dictates what we shall do and think. We become an *it* whose existence is to be used by others. In this inauthentic way of being, we *fall* into the world. The alienation of falling is tempting and tranquilizing. It is only by thinking that we can bring about a better world and discover the meaning that Being holds for us. By learning to keep silent before Being we become intuitively attuned to its mystery.

The relation between the presuppositions of the philosophy and its derived tenants concerning epistemology can be summed up as follows:

Materialism:

> Presupposition: Only sense knowledge is valid.
>
> Question: Considering only sensations as valid, what is the role of the understanding?
>
> Conclusion: It is fallacious; therefore we cannot know truth from falsity.

Immaterialism

> Presupposition: We do our own thinking through reminiscence of universal forms. (Plato)
>
> Question: Since our understanding is of the universal forms, is it true or false?
>
> Conclusion: It must necessarily be true, and falsity is left unexplained.

Traditional Philosophy

> Presupposition: Reason gives us objective truth about reality.
>
> Question: What is the role of the understanding?
>
> Conclusion: To arrive at truth by affirming that which is and negating that which is not, according to first principles of being.

Contemporary Philosophy

> Presupposition: We relate to Being through the principles of lived experience.
>
> Question: What are the principles of lived experience by which we relate to Being?
>
> Conclusion: By living authentically and by sharing in the thinking, we dis-cover Being.

1. Hume, *Enquiry Concerning Human Understanding* from *Essential Works*, p. 51. Author's italics

2. Ibid., p. 167

3. Berkeley, *Selections*, p. 118

4. Kurt Goldstein, *Human Nature in the Light of Psychopathology* (Cambridge, Massachusetts: Harvard University Press, 1940), p. 60 (parenthesis added)

5. Bernard J. F. Lonergan, *Insight* (New York: Harper & Row, 1978), p. 552

6. Thomas Aquinas quoting Augustine, *De Veritate*, 21, 6

7. Goldstein, *Human Nature ...*, p. 77

8. Ibid., pp. 46-47

9. Ibid., pp. 47-8

10. Henri Bergson, *Time and Free Will*, F. L. Pogson (New York: Harper & Row, 1960), p. 106

11. James, *Pragmatism*, p. 118

12. Heidegger, *Being and Time*, p. 191

13. Goldstein, *Human ...*, p. 66

14. Martin Heidegger, *What Is Philosophy?* trans. W. Kluback and J. Wilde (New York: Twayne Publishers, 1958), p. 49

15. Martin Heidegger, *What Is Called Thinking?* trans. F. D. Wieck and J. G. Gray (New York: Harper & Row, 1968), p. 28

16. Heidegger, *Being and Time*, p. 213

17. Ibid., p. 217

18. Ibid., p. 164

19. Ibid. p. 220

20. Ibid., p. 223

21. Ibid., p. 85

22. Martin Heidegger, *Introduction to Metaphysics*, trans. R. Manheim (New Haven: Yale University Press, 1959), p. 116

23. Ibid., p. 116

24. Martin Heidegger, *The Question Concerning Technology*, trans. W. Lovitt (New York: Harper & Row, 1977), p. 55

25. Claude Bragdon *The Eternal Poles* (New York: Alfred A. Knopf, 1931), p. 103

Chapter IV

THE DIMENSION OF WORLD

The presuppositions of a particular philosophy affect the way we understand and thus form our world. Materialism or relativism contends that we perceive only sensations of physical objects, acts, or places. Therefore we have only an environment rather than a world. Berkeley's form of immaterialism says that what we call reality is merely sensations that are clearly perceived which have no existence outside of mind. Traditional philosophy posits the world as "objectively out there" with the human person standing against it as subject. Contemporary philosophy would agree with none of these but draws attention to the fact that the world cannot be known apart from the knower and yet it is not we who create world. The world worlds itself independently of us. Nor are we subjects standing against an objective world, but we ourselves and world can be understood only in terms of that which grounds us both, i.e., Being.

Though the world is one, there are as many different world-models as there are persons to create them. The following illustrates the contrast in world-views. A pygmy, living all of his life in tall grass country, was accustomed to seeing everything in short perspective. A visiting scientist brought him to see the plains for the first time, pointing out bison grazing in the distance. But since the bison were visible at his eye level, as well as diminished in size because of their distance, the pygmy mistook them for insects. Unless we can understand how the other forms his world, e.g., see the world through his eyes, we cannot expect to be able to communicate with him.

Because each person's world entails a projection into the future, there cannot be any single correct grasp of the totality that is world. Each model needs to be completed by other world-models. Plato, for example, through his dialectical thinking, made many discoveries of the possibilities that Being holds for us by bringing justice to bear on human affairs. However, with his theory of forms he diminished the value of creativity by seeing the created work as merely a copy of a copy, i.e., a copy of a sensible object which, in turn, is merely a copy of a universal form. It was left to later generations to fill in this missing dimension.

Nor are any of our differing world-models fixed and stable. We are constantly correcting and expanding our world-model, as we should be if we are to grow in understanding. Every breakthrough increases the foresight needed to meet our own needs as well as the needs of future generations. What we do not only affects our own country but other countries as well, e.g., acid rain. We have an obligation to future generations to care for the inheritance we have received from past generations.

Our actions are influenced by the weight that we give to various facets of our world. In determining how to formulate world, it is important to know how our knowledge affects our actions and vice versa. Unless we understand the possibilities of our being, we will not put forth the effort necessary to actuate them. On the other hand, it is essential to understand the limitations placed upon us in order that we plan realistically and do not encroach on other person's rights. We are not suggesting a pragmatic approach, however. The way we formulate world grows out of our understanding of Being, and this includes not only the practical but that which transcends everydayness, i.e., the mystery of Being. By understanding the various ways that world can be formulated, we are enabled to decide for ourselves which will be more fruitful. Examining the consequences of each world-view gives us an opportunity to originate a more adequate world-model.

Unless we are aware of the bias with which we form our world we will be held fast by one point of view and become shortsighted in respect to others. The pragmatist William James, attempting to overcome the tendency to ignore the subjective element in the creation of our world-model, points out that we unwittingly let our personality type determine the content and bias of our philosophy. Instead of thinking through the question of what it means to be, we have a tendency to adhere to those precepts which are most familiar to us or which justify our actions.

James lists the characteristics of two personality types which demonstrate extreme opposite philosophical positions. The tough-minded is typical of materialism and the tender-minded is characteristic of immaterialism. These define the parameters of possible world-views but, as extreme views, represent merely an incomplete sampling of being.[1]

The Dimension of World

Tough-minded	*Tender-minded*
Materialist (mechanistic)	(Immaterialist) idealist
Empiricist (only experience has validity)	Rationalist (only reason has validity)
Sensationalistic (only sensations accepted)	Intellectualist (strict adherence to principles)
Pessimistic (the worst of all possible worlds)	Optimistic (the best of all possible worlds)
Irreligious (religion is a crutch)	Religious (fundamentalist or formalist)
Fatalistic (determinist)	(Liberalistic) (licentious)
Pluralistic (all beings are different)	Monistic (all being is the same)
Skeptical (doubts validity of reason)	Dogmatic (accepts authority uncritically)
Relativist[2] (elite measures values)	Absolutist (authority determines values)

James warns against mixing these views. Ordinary people, says James, wish to choose by hit and miss from both philosophies. We are or should be

> vexed by too much inconsistency and vacillation in our creed. We cannot preserve a good intellectual conscience so long as we keep mixing incompatibles from opposite sides of the line.[3]

It would be inconsistent, for example, to contend with materialism that only sense knowledge is valid and then to believe in God or to adhere to principles when neither can be sensed.

But even more important is to realize that, the tender-minded and the tough-minded are each contradictory in relation to reality. To adhere to either one is to live a contradiction, e.g., Hume, though spurning intellectual knowledge, uses his intellect to expose his theory. Socrates made the point that any extreme philosophy inevitably turns into its opposite - if we think according to one extreme, we will discover ourselves acting according to the other extreme, e.g., too much freedom turns into anarchy. To live by contradiction causes us either to reject our behavior or to lose faith in our capacity to discover truth. It is possible to overcome this limitation by understanding the relation between precepts and derived conclusions.

The extremes of materialism/immaterialism might be called tunnel vision since the parameters of the world-view are so constricted that one's possibilities of action are unduly limited. The contradictions inherent in either one lead to a curtailment of world and consequently of our sphere of action. Traditional and contemporary philosophy, on the other hand, reconcile the two opposites, revealing the profound possibilities Being offers us.

Traditional and contemporary philosophy sustain a middle way between the opposites of materialism and immaterialism. They represent a higher third because they include all of the benefits of the extremes, but in due measure, so that they lead to actions which are rational, profound, and sincere. This coincidence of opposites avoids the error of materialism which reduces man to an animal and his world to a mere environment, thereby encouraging only half-hearted effort toward the realization of his never-to-be discovered possibilities. Nor, on the other hand, does it lose itself and its freedom, as does immaterialism, in a frenzy of seeking the perfectionism of an ideal. It is the middle way which recognizes the possible and varied dimensions of the human person, allowing him a full measure of freedom to form his world in a manner fitting to his peculiar talents and in full consideration of whatever the world offers him in the way of opportunity. It is philosophy which clarifies the following differences in the way world is formed. As Plato pointed out, Eros, or love, ascends to the beauty of the forms, which is the way of wisdom, i.e., philosophy. James notes that although philosophy "bakes no bread" and to common people it seems to be always quibbling, doubting, or challenging, yet "no one of us can get along without the far-flashing beams of light it sends over the world's perspectives."[4]

A Materialist Environment

Many philosophers of the West have subscribed to materialism. Among pre-Socratics, the atomists and the Greek philosopher Empedocles believed that knowledge consists solely of sensations which were thought to be caused by an effluence of atoms given off by material objects. Epicurus believed the universe (including human beings) to be governed by the laws of mechanics. Among modern philosophers of the West, Locke, Hume, and Hobbes can be cited as materialists, as well as positivists such as Compte. Nominalism, conceptualism, skepticism, empiricism, and relativism are also reductionist in refusing to recognize any dimension of being other than the physical. Among psychologists, Freud and the behaviorist Skinner are outstanding examples.

What is it like to live in a materialist environment? In order to answer this question, it is necessary to imagine ourselves in the particular framework from which the materialist speaks. Although he may use the same terminology employed by other philosophers, it is used with specific meaning and should be understood in the context intended. On reading Hume, for example, one is often tempted to believe that he posited powers over and above the senses since he often uses such words as *experimental reasoning, ideas, thought, intellect, will,* and so forth. However, Hume leaves no doubt about his use of these words when he asks: From what [sense] impression is that supposed idea derived? He concludes that if it cannot be derived from a particular impression that "our suspicion that it is without meaning is confirmed."[5] Accepting only sensations as valid, he rules out knowledge that begins in the intellect such as philosophy as well as self-reflective knowledge. Nor does he admit to knowledge once removed from sense impressions such as the concept of motion. Knowledge consists solely of images, hence, just as for an animal, this is an environment rather than a world.

According to Hume, our sense impressions only give us knowledge of static entities, consequently there is no motion in a materialistic environment. A stone or metal raised in the air and dropped, says Hume, does not even reveal a downward or upward motion or "any other motion in the stone or the metal." Nor is motion passed from one object to another. "Motion in the second Billiard-ball is quite a distinct event from motion in the first."[6] Since the senses retain nothing of motion except the position of the moving body, motion itself is excluded. That we are under the impression motion exists can be explained by the rapid succession of sense images which gives us the feeling of motion, like that which we derive from watching the succession of stills in a motion picture. Jean Piaget notes that the "object permanence" of stills is the way animals and babies under two years of age perceive the external world. For example, in an experiment with Scottie dogs, it was found that if a puppy is allowed to sniff a dish of food at point A, and then taken to point C and held on a leash while he watches the food moved to point B, he will immediately return to point A expecting to find the food where he originally saw it. For Piaget, a child's change from object permanence to object flexibility is the beginning of the human being's ability to understand motion, whereas for Hume motion remains an illusion.

If there is no motion, can there be any action of a cause upon an effect in a materialist environment? Hume makes the questionable observation - since the senses can imagine a cause separate from its effect, the two must be unrelated. There is nothing more to causality than a succession of events. A prior event is called a cause and the posterior event, an effect. Not all sequences of prior/posterior events are referred to as cause/effect, says Hume, but only those which we habitually perceive. "A cause is that after which anything constantly exists." Why does Hume deny real causality? He notes that we have no sense impression of either production or necessary connection, i.e., since a necessary connection is known immaterially, it cannot be seen or otherwise sensed. And since he accepts only material sense knowledge as valid, the idea of a necessary connection between events must be denied.[7] In other words, what we do has no real relation to the effect that follows. A necessary connection between myself and what I produce is merely an illusion. But if causality were merely a sequence of habitually perceived events, we could just as well say that night causes daylight and daylight causes night. According to traditional philosophy, a real cause is that which gives being to an effect. It is not night that causes daylight but the sun which possesses sufficient energy to illuminate the earth. There is a necessary connection between the sun and daylight since, without this particular sun, this particular daylight would not have existed. However, in the materialist environment nothing produces or causes another. Effects are merely fortuitous.

Since, for materialism, it is a mechanistic environment, there are only instrumental causes. Rather than the efficient cause of our own actions, we merely respond to whatever stimulates us the most at the time. It is true that animals act according to Humean causality since their knowledge consists of a sequence of images of prior and posterior events. A dog struck by a truck, for example, thereafter chased trucks. However, in judging real causality, we observe that the truck is merely an instrumental cause since it does not have sufficient being to purposefully steer itself. We look, then, to the efficient cause or driver of the truck as the cause of this accident, since it is he who gives being to the effect. But in a materialist world, all efficient causes are reduced to instrumental causes.

Since in a materialist world there is no efficient causality, there is no self-instigated change. There is an environment but no *world* of possibilities nor the freedom to effectuate these possibilities. Just as animals are only aware of their surroundings but do not formulate a world in which to plan their future and deliberately carry it out, so we, too, according to materialism, are immersed in an environment that determines what we will know and do. This is a very simple way of life since we expend no effort to think and to plan for our future but act instinctively or mechanistically. Since we are not aware of possible being, we are limited to what the environment stimulates us to do at the time.

Since pseudo-causality is the basis of superstition, the materialist world is beset by imaginary evils. With no necessary connection between cause and effect, a black cat crossing our path could just as well be thought to *cause* our *bad luck*. "Man is worse off than other beings," says Hume's character Philo, "because he is the victim of his own superstition."

Since materialism can admit only a form of pseudo-causality, it can provide no basis for science. Science requires knowledge of a necessary connection between cause and effect such that without this cause this particular effect would not occur. For materialism, statistical evidence replaces science. Although statistics give valuable estimations, they do not distinguish between real and pseudo-causes of effects. Mark Twain pokes fun at this reliance upon statistics with his whimsical remark that the most dangerous place to be is in bed since most people die there. Science demands more than statistical correlation. It is known, for example, that statistically there is more turbulent weather during a period of sunspot activity. Yet, since there is no evidence as yet as to why this occurs, it is not accepted by scientists as a necessary cause/effect relationship. Since, for materialism, only sense impressions are accepted as a valid form of knowledge, science cannot be admitted.

Since materialism excludes immaterial knowledge, it also curtails the meaning of the word *being*. *Being* can be used merely as a name, indicating the presence of material entities, e.g., being here rather than being there. This is strictly a physical environment. Because materialism cannot affirm our existence, the possibility of our coming-to-be or passing away likewise has no meaning. Nor can we transcend our immediate environment to attain to greater possibilities.

What do philosophers of materialism say about their environment? Are they optimistic and pleased with what life has to offer? Hume says through the character of Demea:

> And why should man pretend to an exemption from the lot of all other animals? The whole earth, believe me, Philo, is cursed and polluted. A perpetual war is kindled amongst all living creatures. Necessity, hunger, want, stimulate the

> strong and courageous: Fear, anxiety, terror agitate the weak and infirm.[8]

There seems to be no escape from the cursed world for either the strong or the weak. As William James notes, pessimism seems to be the outcome of materialism. The contemporary behaviorist Skinner, in his book, *Beyond Freedom and Dignity*, although envisioning utopian societies effectuated through operant conditioning, finally concludes in his later years that he does not see any hope for the world. Throughout history men have assumed they initiate their own actions but to suppose this is a great mistake. Since Skinner denies self-initiated change, there can be no hope for the future. We are subject to whatever evil our environment foists upon us.

If the world is in such dire condition, where is justice to rectify some of the ills? The word *justice* is used over and over again by materialists. What is the meaning they ascribe to this word? Hume notes that if we all had every conceivable material good we could wish for, there would be no need for justice. But this would be an impossibility since there would always be those who would want to have another person's possessions. If, on the other hand, many were in such a state of poverty that their life depended upon theft, there would also be no justice. He says:

> It will readily, I believe, be admitted that the strict laws of justice are suspended, in such a pressing emergency, and give place to the stronger motives of necessity and self-preservation.[9]

In either extreme of want or abundance, *justice is rendered totally useless.* Since in an environment of material entities all motives center around the acquiring of goods rather than upon human rights, this pseudo-justice has meaning only in reference to property. If one group possesses all of the wealth and the other group is reduced to act according to the instinct of self-preservation, justice is rendered obsolete. But is it not possible that in such dire need just laws could be effective in correcting such a situation? Hume does not consider this option. Nor does he consider that in times of abundance justice is still needed to ensure human rights, such as the right to vote.

Why is materialism only able to substantiate a form of pseudo-justice? "It is a pluralistic world," says the pragmatist William James. Each being is discrete. There is no common essence among beings, but each thing is altogether different from every other. The only manner of joining one thing to another is by similarity of physical appearance or by contiguity in time or space. Sense knowledge reveals no common nature or essence that would set human beings apart from vegetative or animal life. But if we cannot determine the essence of a human being, there will be no basis for human rights and, in turn, no basis for justice: human being=human rights=justice. Those in power could exclude those who have a different physical appearance or are from a different region from participating in government. Hume says that if there were a group of men who, though rational, were inferior in strength of body and mind, we should not render justice to them nor give them rights or property. "The restraints of justice and property, being totally *useless*, would never have place in so unequal a confederacy."[10]

Since, for Hume, there are no natural human rights, it belongs to those in power to determine what laws should prevail and what rights granted. This is pseudo-justice since it is not based on human nature but on superiority. It excludes all those of different race from possessing rights because of their so-called inferiority. Hume gives as an example: "the great superiority of civilized *Europeans* above barbarous *Indians*."[11] Although Hume speaks of *natural law*, Willey points out that the term *natural* as used by Hume does not refer to that which is *original* to human nature but to that which is approved of by the *elite*, the educated men in all *civilized* nations.[12]

Is equality of women observed in such an environment? Hume answers this question: "Nature has given *man* the superiority above *woman*, by endowing him with greater strength both of mind and body... ."[13] (Intelligence tests now reveal that there is no difference in the intelligence of male and female.) Hume does not mean that the English gentleman should not give deference to woman. "It is his part to alleviate that superiority, as much as possible, by the generosity of his behavior."[14] He objects to civilizations that reduce females to the most abject slavery, beating them, and selling them, and so forth. Man in more civilized societies "discover their authority in a more generous, though not a less evident manner ..."[15]

Hobbes, also a materialist, believed that, although there is no natural servitude of one man to another, the child is subject to the parents and likewise the wife to the husband. There is no question of the rights or the dignity of women since this is a materialist environment where physical strength is the sign of superiority.

Since the human being is considered solely in his physical dimension as an entity no different in kind from other material beings, materialism is held by some philosophers to be reductionist. The uniqueness of the human person as well as infinite Being is either overlooked or rejected as meaningless. But if this theory so drastically narrows the meaning of our being, why then do we concern ourselves with it? In order to understand others as well as to clarify our own thoughts, we need to be aware of these divergent world-views. Each person is free to choose the philosophy he wishes to live by, although many persons may not realize that his chosen philosophy may give rise to kinds of actions he or she didn't bargain for. Adamczewski points out that since materialism experiences and manipulates entities "without sounding wherein they are grounded," it is forgetful of being and therefore lacks depth. Yet even such preoccupation "with entities and forgetfulness of being cannot be complete and ultimate if fundamentally some awareness of being - *eksistenz* - is what determines the being of man."[16] Although Hume and other materialists deny any meaning to the word *being*, their very denial requires recognition of that which they deny. Heidegger notes that Being lets all that is, be, and each of us as spokesman for Being says what he can of Being, either by manifesting it or by denying it. Parmenides and Plato consider emphasis upon the senses to be the way of the common man and the Indian Upanishads point to the senses as the first step in the four-fold path to self-knowledge.

The Ideal World of Immaterialism

Although not representing such an extreme position as Berkeley's, other idealists such as Plato, Spinoza, and Hegel, as well as Stoics such as

Epictetus and Marcus Aurelius could be called tender-minded since their world-view leans toward an ideal rather than real world. Though Berkeley contends there is nothing external to mind, idealists believe that, though there are sense perceptions of a real world, it is an ideal world toward which all should strive. Idealism may take the extreme form of adherence to an "ism" such as communism, socialism, and so forth in which passive obedience is demanded.

The immaterialist world-view of Berkeley was an attempt to counteract the atheism of materialism. Since materialism provides no foundation for belief in infinite Being, Berkeley attempted to overcome this shortcoming by over-emphasizing the spiritual dimension of the human person, making the mind completely dependent upon God in order to be and to operate.

In far eastern philosophies, immaterialism represents an attempt to escape the unfortunate conditions of their world by undermining its reality. The Yogacara School of Vasabandu, for example, which later became Hsuan Tsang's Consciousness-Only School, demonstrates its similarity to Berkeley's immaterialism by the following: the true scriptures declare that

> in the three worlds there is nothing but mind, that objects are but a manifestation of consciousness-only, that all dharmas are not separated from the mind, that sentient beings become pure or impure in accordance with the mind, that bodhisattvas (saints of the Mahayana) who perfected the Four Wisdoms will, following their awakening, penetrate the truth of consciousness-only and the absence of spheres of objects.[17]

Vasabandu, like Berkeley, expresses the idea that those who believe in reality external to the mind are as one in a dream and must awaken to the *reality* of consciousness-only. Hsuan-Tsang, unlike Berkeley, however, does not depend upon God to furnish the dharmas (sensations); rather the dharmas themselves *perfume* consciousness. Berkeley contends that because we receive sensations passively, it is God who creates them.

> Sensible things cannot exist otherwise than in a mind or spirit .... Seeing they depend not on my thought, and have an existence distinct from being perceived by me... so sure is there an infinite omnipresent Spirit who contains and supports it (the sensible world).[18]

However, as Yogacara realized, just because we receive them passively does not mean that it is God who is the cause of them.

Since Berkeley's presupposition is that minds and the thoughts and the sensations that minds perceive are the only reality, that which we call real does not exist externally to the mind. Berkeley must call upon "another Will or Spirit that produces them ... the admirable connexion whereof sufficiently testifies to the wisdom and benevolence of its Author." In other words, since there is no external world to produce sensations, they must be created by God. This gives us but one of two choices, neither of which is satisfactory. First, if God creates our sense images then we ourselves cannot act as secondary causes, producing an object according to our own design. We would be powerless to effectuate any changes in the world since our sense impressions would not be influenced by our own causality. For example, if we believed we were taking action to clean up our environment, it would be God, not us, who would be improving it. On the other hand, by claiming the work is ours, we would be dictating to God what he must give us in the way of sensations. Immaterialism thus either claims too much power for the human person to be realistic or too little power for us to be effective causes.

According to Berkeley, since it is God who creates our sense impressions, they must be perfect. Berkeley says in the voice of Philonus:

> Look! are not the fields covered with a delightful verdure? Is there not something in the woods and groves, in the rivers and clear springs that soothes, that delights, that transports the soul? ... Even in rocks and deserts is there not an agreeable wildness! How sincere a pleasure is it to behold the natural beauties of the earth.[19]

This is an optimistic world-view. The world is as it is because God decreed it, according to Berkeley; therefore we should not attempt to change it. Whatever God decrees is a General Law of Nature, and although the world may appear to be calamitous, nevertheless, it is the best that can be, because God made it. It is up to us to perceive it to be so. Berkeley says:

> All kinds of calamities public and private, do arise from a uniform steady observation of those General Laws which are once established by the Author of Nature, and which He will not change or deviate from upon any of those accounts....[20]

If God will not deviate from the world order he has created, neither should we decide to protest or change the world, but we should accept it passively. Immaterialism thus opts for passive obedience to God or to whomever is the elect of God, e.g., the divine right of kings. Whereas active obedience requires one to judge whether a command is just before obeying it, passive obedience requires no justification but follows authority blindly.

When any philosophy is extremist, it turns into its opposite. Thus a completely immaterialist philosophy gives rise to actions that are characteristic of a materialist philosophy and vice versa. An enigmatic feature of this turning is that one believes he is opposing the contradictory viewpoint, whereas he acts in correspondence with it. For example, the absolutism of immaterialism turns over authority to the *elect*, whether of a religious creed or an *ism* such as communism. With the same result, the relativism of materialism contends that law is without basis in reality and consists merely in consent to contractual legality which in practice results in a rule of the elite, arbitrarily set up in favor of those laws which further private interests. In either case, the human person loses his freedom to plan his world and to actuate his many dimensions. In this and many other instances, there is a turning of an extreme view into its opposite. This turning is made evident in the following Taoist symbol in which the black dot on the white ground will increase until it becomes its opposite just as the white dot will take over the shaded ground. The enclosing circle represents the coincidence of opposites found in traditional and contemporary philosophy.

The World-view of Traditional Philosophy

The world-view of traditional philosophy is neither pessimistic nor euphoric but a coincidence of the opposites of materialism and immaterialism in which the high esteem that man has for truth keeps him in touch with a real world. He fortifies himself with the faith and hope necessary to cope with the tragedies of life, and in gratitude and respect, appreciates the good bestowed on him.

The presupposition of traditional philosophy is that the world can be known objectively through reason. What can reason tell us about the universe? The conclusion is that the universe consists of a hierarchy of beings of increasing complexity from non-living beings to the most complex creature of all which is the human being. Each more complex form of being includes within itself the less complex forms of being. Aristotle distinguishes between the living and the non-living. The living is further specified as either vegetative or animal life, the former being characterized by its cellular activity and the latter, in addition, by the possession of sense organs which enable it to determine its own means to a predetermined end. The human being not only has self-movement and determines his own action, but unlike other forms of life, moves himself toward an end of his own choosing. Virtually possessing chemical, vegetative, and animal life, the human person is nevertheless specifically a rational being, possessing immaterial as well as material powers.

Traditional philosophy gives us a majestic world-view that looks to God or infinite Being as the creator of our being. It could be said to be symbolized in the cathedral which points its spires heavenward and by its grandeur inspires man to transcend himself. Leaning toward the tender-minded, it fosters development of the many dimensions of the human person but always within ethical guidelines and with a tendency to regulate human conduct by universal principles rather than by consideration for individual preferences. It is a structured world, the human being looking to government as the authority in civil life and to religion as the source of spiritual sustenance. It recognizes the coming-to-be of human beings as the created effects of the uncaused Cause. The infinite Being is perceived as primary Cause; yet human beings are effective secondary causes. Traditional philosophy establishes our spiritual dimension by a rational appraisal of those acts which are uniquely human and emphasizes man's natural desire to transcend this world in the dimensionless dimension of eternal life.

Whereas traditional philosophy looks to real causality for an explanation of reality, thus ushering in the scientific revolution, contemporary philosophy sees that traditional philosophy's over-emphasis on real causality has led science to discover, not only how to improve the world, but how to destroy it. Although everything has its reasons, not everything can be known through causality. We now need the guidance of that which transcends science.

The Worlding of World
According to Contemporary Philosophy

One important difference between traditional and contemporary philosophy is that the former perceives man as subject standing outside of the world as object. Contemporary philosophy overcomes the subject/object dichotomy by perceiving man as primordially in-the-world-with-others. Heidegger typifies the traditional notion of man and world as the time of the world-picture, in which man as subject need only passively perceive the universe, stretching out before him as picture. In contrast, contemporary philosophy perceives the relation of man to world as active involvement. Man must create his own world-model by which to realize his destiny.

As the ground of our being and the being of world, Being gives us to ourselves and worlds world. By dis-covering this ground we become aware of our act of forming our world and realize at the same time the worldhood of world, i.e., that it is as it is and not otherwise. World becomes more accessible as Being discloses itself to us, making it possible for us to actuate our many dimensions.

Being reveals itself through world inasmuch as we are aware of the existence of that-which-is-in-totality. We could never know the sum total of all beings, the totality-of-that-which-is, and therefore an environment must always be limited. But with our immaterial power we can understand and relate to that-which-is-in-totality, i.e., Being. Our relation to Being is made explicit by the way we formulate our world, says Heidegger.[21] "Entering a world happens with Being." It is Being that is constitutive of Dasein. As the horizon of Being, world exceeds the boundaries of the actual to encompass the far greater extent of the possible. Through the planning of our *destiny*, we permeate world and world permeates us. World is essentially for the sake of, whether for the sake of ourselves or for the sake of others. We have being-in-the-world in such a way that we can understand ourselves as bound up in our destiny with the being of those entities we encounter within the world.[22]

We relate ourselves to other beings-in-the-world through concern. Attending to something, letting something go, interrogating, and considering are ways of concern for our world. The opposite of these, leaving undone, neglecting, renouncing, taking a rest, these, too, are ways of concern, says Heidegger "but these are deficient modes, in which the possibilities of concern are reduced to a bare minimum."[23] We relate to those things that are at-hand through care. We have care for the present-at-hand of nature through concern for its conservation or, in a deficient mode, by its useless destruction. We have care for the ready-to-hand of tools through concern for their skillful handicrafting and proper use or, in a deficient mode, by our becoming a slave to technocracy.

According to Heidegger, in this age of technology, equipment and tools have gained priority over nature, i.e., because of mechanization Dasein has lost its intimacy with nature and, consequently, with God. Though Being at one time revealed itself to man through its created effects, Dasein has, for the most part, closed its eyes and ears to the beautiful design of material things and, consequently, to its designer. The intimacy between man and nature provided the basis for man's belief in an eternal spirit, i.e., God, as is revealed in the prayer of an American Indian.

An Indian Prayer

O' Great Spirit,
Whose voice I hear in the winds,
And whose breath gives life to all the world,
hear me! I am small and weak. I need your
strength and wisdom.

Let Me Walk In Beauty, and make my eyes
ever behold the red and purple sunset.

Make My Hands respect the things you have
made and my ears sharp to hear your voice.

Make Me Wise so that I may understand the
things you have taught my people.

Let Me Learn the lessons you have hidden
in every leaf and rock.

I Seek Strength, not to be greater than my
brother, but to fight my greatest
enemy -- myself.

Make Me Always Ready to come to you with
clean hands and straight eyes.

So When Life Fades, *as the fading sunset,*
my spirit may come to you
without shame.[24]

With the outstanding progress of science, man arrogantly looks upon himself rather than upon infinite Being as creator so that in this age Being has become covered over and hidden. Hopefully, by taking thought for the ground of our being, we can uncover Being and, with the interpenetration of Dasein and Being, find our way in this age.

We are thrown into a world not of our own choosing. We are aware of our facticity, that it is we who are here in the world as it is. We were born into a particular region, with particular parents, and so forth beyond our control. We did not choose the particular talents we were born with nor do we have control over the possibilities that society offers or refuses us. Nevertheless we cannot evasively turn away from our facticity. By learning to accept our *thrownness* we can overcome or compensate for the limitations of our facticity and move ahead to actualize our possibilities.

To what extent do we, ourselves, determine how world presents itself? Do we determine how world appears to us and thus also determine what our action will be in response to world? Or is world pre-determined? As a coincidence of opposites, world is neither relative nor is it predetermined. World worlds itself and yet Dasein's world is personal insofar as it pertains to the possibilities and destiny of Dasein. Dasein's role in the forming of its world is made clear by Heidegger: The essence of its being is such that it itself *forms its world*, in the sense that it lets world happen and through the world provides itself with an original view (form) which does not grasp explicitly, yet serves as a model for, all of manifest being, Dasein included.[25] Although we *form* world, we do not create a make-believe world. By letting world be as it is, we provide ourselves with a model which gives meaning to our world and allows us to realize our destiny. In the state-of-mind of mood, we are brought face to face with the *there* of our existence. "A mood makes manifest *how one is* and *how one is faring*," says Heidegger, e.g., boredom denotes failure to open ourselves to our possibilities (the error of materialism) whereas frustration indicates a world-model with contradictory possibilities (the error of immaterialism).

Since we are beings-in-the-world-with-others, it is the responsibility of each of us to alert himself or herself to the problems facing the world community and to take concrete steps to correct them. We should be even now doing our part, however, seemingly insignificant, to allieviate the suffering caused by, e.g., abuse of human rights. Martin Luther King noted that injustice anywhere is a threat to justice everywhere. Prejudice against race, old age, and so forth, drugs, starvation, and homelessness testify to misuse of our human potentiality. Economic crises such as personal and governmental over-spending is leading to a burgeoning national debt. Such disasters as massive deforestation, destruction of wild life and pollution are increasing at such a rapid rate that we are turning our earthly home into a wasteland. By participating in the fullness of Being, we can avert these threats and form a world-model that will increase the standard of living for all.

Summary

The environment of the materialist and the *world* of the immaterialist define the parameters of possible world-views. Each provides us with only a partial sampling of being, offering us very little opportunity to realize our many dimensions. Materialism admits only the physical dimension of the human person with the result that we are conceived as one among many static entities with no potentiality for change and exercising no real causality. Man, like an animal, is merely an instrumental cause with no purpose or future. The outlook for this world-view is pessimistic since we possess no power by which we could improve our environment. Nor is there any possibility of transcending this environment since the only dimension is the material.

The immaterialist world, on the other hand, is idealist and perfectionist. The external world is a misconception and the only reality is mind and its perceptions. Since God creates our sense images, it must be a perfect world. Natural disasters are according to the will of God and should be accepted passively. Truth is whatever can be known clearly; hence the mystery of Being is ruled out. Our causality does not extend beyond our own mind. We cannot bring about changes in the real world but only in our world-view. Submissive acceptance of authority is the norm.

Traditional and contemporary philosophy represent a coincidence of the opposites of materialism and immaterialism in which is realized the many dimensions of the human person. Traditional philosophy offers us a world-picture in which man stands as subject passively viewing the universe as object. This universe takes into account both identity and difference. Neither the uniqueness of the human person is sacrificed nor his common essence with other beings. The world manifests a hierarchy of beings of increasing complexity. The human person shares with other beings his chemical, vegetative, and animal make-up but is unique as a being who is rational. All beings are created by infinite Being or God and, as a secondary cause, the human person shares in God's creative power.

Contemporary philosophy sees Dasein as the one to whom Being presences itself. We become conscious of ourselves in terms of our world. World belongs to selfhood. We are coming-to-be- in-the-midst-of-the-world in everydayness. Our destiny is bound up with other beings-in-the- world, with the present-at-hand of nature, the ready-to-hand of tools, and in solicitude toward other Dasein. Whereas in other times, Being revealed itself through nature, in this age of technocracy, Being is covered over. By taking thought we can un-cover Being, realizing once again our oneness with Being.

Being worlds world independently of Dasein, consequently, it is not a relative world. World is thrown over Being. By forming our own world-model, we interpenetrate Being and Being makes itself manifest to us. The interplay of Being and Dasein is not only the necessary condition of world but of world inextricably and unavoidably personal. The authenticity of our world-model is revealed in mood, which makes us aware of the truth and appropriateness of our world-model. By letting Being be, we form for ourselves a true manifestation of world and, realizing our destiny, transcend our own finiteness to open the way toward experiencing Being itself.

The relation between the presuppositions of the philosophy and its derived tenants concerning world can be summed up thus:

Materialism

Presupposition: Only sensations have validity.

Question: Since only sensations have validity, what can be known about the world?

Conclusion: There is only an environment with no world of possibilities and no hope for the future.

Immaterialism

>Presupposition: God gives us sensations of a *real world.*

>Question: Since God gives us our sensations, what effect does this have on the *real world?*

>Conclusion: It is a perfect world but over which we have no control.

Traditional Philosophy

>Presupposition: We know world objectively through reason.

>Question: What does reason tell us about the universe?

>Conclusion: The universe is made up of a hierarchy of finite beings of which God is primary cause and man secondary cause.

Contemporary philosophy

>Presupposition: The principles of my lived experience demonstrate my relation to world.

>Question: How do the principles of my lived experience reveal world?

>Conclusion: Letting world be as it is and not otherwise, I form a world-model, planning my destiny.

1. William James, *Pragmatism* (Cambridge: Harvard University Press, 1979), p. 13. (parentheses added)

2. Added by author

3. James, *Pragmatism*, p. 14

4. Ibid., pp. 10-11

5. David Hume, *An Enquiry Concerning Human Understanding* from *The Essential Works of David Hume*, ed. R. Cohen (New York: Bantam Books, 1965), p. 56

6. Ibid., p. 65

7. David Hume, *A Treatise of Human Nature* from *Philosophical Works*, ed. T. H. Green and T. H. Grose, 4 vols. (London: Scientia Verlag Aalen, 1964), I, 457

8. David Hume, "Dialogues Concerning Natural Religion," *Essential Works*, p. 359

9. David Hume, "An Enquiry Concerning the Principles of Moral," *Essential Works*, p. 192

10. Ibid., p. 196

11. Ibid

12. A. J. Beitzinger, "Hume's Aristocratic Preference," *Review of Politics*, Vol. 28 #2 (Apr., 1966), p. 171

13. Hume, *Essential Works*, p. 438

14. Ibid.

15. Ibid.

16. Zygmunt Adamczewski, "Questions in Heidegger's Thought About Being," from *The Question of Being* (University Park: Pennsylvania State University Press, 1978), p. 59

17. Wing-Tsit Chan, trans. "The Treatise on the Establishment of the Doctrine of Consciousness Only," *A Source Book in Chinese Philosophy*, (Princeton: Princeton University Press, 1963), p. 387

18. George Berkeley, *Three Dialogues between Hylas and Philonus* in *Berkeley, Essay, Principles, Dialogues*, ed. M. W. Calkins (New York: Charles Scribner's Sons, 1957), p. 276

19. Ibid., p. 274

20. Berkeley, "Passive Obedience," from *Berkeley, Essay ...*, p. 438

21. Martin Heidegger, *Being and Time*, trans. J. Macquarrie and E. Robinson (Oxford: Basil Blackwell, 1967), p. 92

22. Ibid., pp. 82-83

23. Martin Heidegger, *The Essence of Reasons*, ed. J. Wild and J. Edie (Evanston: Northwestern University Press, 1969), p. 89

24. A gift from the Sioux Indian children of Red Cloud Indian School, Holy Rosary Mission, Pine Ridge, South Dakota 57770

25. Heidegger, *Essence of Reasons*, p. 89

Chapter V

DIMENSIONS OF FREEDOM, CREATIVITY, AND PLAY

If we were to ask ourselves what is the most important asset that we possess as human beings, we would very likely answer that it is our power to be free. Freedom has never been experienced or treasured as much as it is today. Yet not all persons are so fortunate as to experience the full extent of their freedom. Rollo May tells a little story about a man who lost his freedom and the effect it had upon him.[1]

> A whimsical king decided one day that he would enjoy seeing what effect it would have if a man were to lose his freedom. An ordinary man, who was on his way to work, was taken captive by the king's men and put into a cage in the royal courtyard. Since he was accustomed to being free, the man was at first bewildered and demanded to be released so that he wouldn't be late to work. When he at last realized that he was not to regain his freedom, his bewilderment changed to anger. This kept his spirits up for a while, but when he was chided by the king for complaining, he became very cynical. As time wore on, he attempted to adjust to his situation, even trying to convince those who visited him that this was a good thing. But his hope withered and he lapsed into silence. Finally, he became insane.

With the loss of his freedom, Being no longer had any meaning for him. In everydayness we take our freedom for granted to such an extent that it is difficult for us to realize how dull and pointless our life would be without freedom. But, if we do not understand and protect our freedom, we are always in danger of losing it, not because some king might put us in a cage, but because we, ourselves, might do so, like a person who, facing away from the only door open to him, remains forever in his cell rather than turning about and walking out of it. The question we are now faced with is whether or not the following philosophies provide the basis necessary for freedom.

Is Freedom Possible in a Materialist Environment?

Materialism says that all of our desires are a result of sense appetite, instinct, or conditioning. Just as an animal is stimulated to move toward a particular goal, so man is necessitated to act on whatever stimulates him the most at the time. Rather than providing incentive for finding a higher good to pursue, for Hume, the sole purpose of sense knowledge is to serve the passions. Without immaterial powers, man is not free to choose his own ends nor initiate his own acts but must obey his instincts.

Freud takes a materialist position when he equates man with animal, denying the ego freedom to act or not act. The id as the seat of desire makes its claim upon the ego which is necessitated to carry out the demands of the id and can at most delay its satisfaction or sublimate its desires. Comparing the ego to a rider on his horse (the id), Freud says the ego

> in its relation to the id is like a man on horseback, who has to hold in check the superior strength of the horse; with this difference, that the rider tries to do so with his own strength while the ego uses borrowed forces.... Often a rider, if he is not to be parted from his horse, is obliged to guide it where it wants to go; so in the same way the ego is in the habit of transforming the id's will into action as if it were its own.[2]

The "borrowed forces" of the ego are the totems and taboos of the superego which reinforce or deter the pleasure principle of the id. In other words, for Freud, we are either necessitated by the pleasure principle (the id) or by the super-ego which forces the ego to comply by means of reward or punishment. Since these totems and taboos are norms set up by parents, society, and so forth, our actions are not initiated by an independent decision. The ego is caught between the super-ego and the id and cannot determine its own actions. Because of its presupposition, that only sense knowledge is valid, materialism negates the immaterial powers by which freedom is made possible.

Dimensions of Freedom, Creativity, and Play

The Epicureans, realizing their materialism denies freedom of decision, attempted to remedy this deficit by explaining that the mechanistic atoms that compose all things are sometimes interrupted by a fortuitous spontaneous action. They believed that this "swerve" in nature explains how a human being is not completely determined but to a certain extent has free choice. However, freedom to act or not act requires self-determined action and since the "swerve" is accidental rather than deliberate, it cannot be free.

Hume also tried to add free choice to his materialism, but James criticizes Hume's "soft determinism" as pure sophistry. Materialism and freedom are contradictory since, for materialism, choice is motivated by instinct. It is not deliberate and consequently not free. When an animal acts it is in response to a sufficient stimulus. With two competing stimuli the stronger one will prevail. If it does not act it is because the stimulus is not sufficient to move the animal. The materialist Hobbes gives us an example of the kind of argument used by a materialist to deny freedom. He says that since all psychological processes are modifications of the brain, human action follows the same laws as mechanical motion and, since nothing mechanical is self-starting, no human action is free. But this argument is circular since it begins by reducing the human person to his psychological processes and then reduces psychological processes to mechanics and on the basis of mechanics claims that man has no freedom. But to compare the human person to a machine is reductionist.

The behaviorist B. F. Skinner is also consistent with materialism in advising that human beings be conditioned just as one would condition an animal. For example, some penologists have assumed that persons who disobey the law can be made to comply with social norms through positive or negative reinforcement. At the Iowa Security Medical Facility, inmates who committed infractions like lying or swearing were given a shot of apomorphine, causing violent vomiting for fifteen minutes or more. Whether effective or not, the courts objected to such treatment.

> The Eighth Circuit Court of Appeals declared that Iowa's use of vomit-inducing apomorphine was cruel and unusual punishment - and therefore unconstitutional - unless the

inmate gives knowing written consent which can be revoked at any time.[3]

The conclusion reached is that human beings, unlike animals, cannot be conditioned against their will. If consented to, the behavior modification programs "have some fairly good rate of success with volunteers, but they have a very low record of success with non-volunteers."[4] Contrary to Skinner, human beings cannot be effectively treated without their free consent.

Our contemporary court system, which allows the release of many indicted criminals, is subject to what James refers to as "hard determinism," the belief that no man can determine his own behavior but is subject to the conditioning of his environment. Although a poor environment has a deleterious effect on some persons, environment in itself is not a sufficient cause of crime. Many law-abiding citizens come from poor neighborhoods and yet are motivated either to correct such conditions or to find another place to live. Heredity also plays a role in our actions but does not necessitate us. Although identical twins have very similar talents and bodily dispositions, statistics show that twins raised together are more dissimilar than those raised apart. The ability to exercise one's freedom outweighs both heredity and environment.

What is it like to live in a materialist environment without freedom? If we believe that we are necessitated to act in a particular way because of forces beyond our control, we will be indifferent to values. It would be pointless for us to set up a value system for ourselves if we see that we are at the mercy of our instincts or unconscious, or if heredity or environment necessitates us to act in a particular way. Our only reason for obeying social norms would be to avoid punishment. Although Hume contends that the sole purpose of knowledge is to serve the passions, Chu Hsi finds that "thinking can check passionate desire." To live only to serve one's own egotistical ends stifles initiative and leads to pessimism and boredom. The talents and possibilities open to a human being far exceed what is necessary to fill our own physical and mental needs. It is only by reaching out to others that we can realize our full potential. He who develops five talents will be given five more, whereas he who has only one talent but clings to it, refusing to use it to help others will lose even that one.

Freedom as License
According to Immaterialism

Since immaterialism contends that we do our own thinking and possess an immaterial will with which we can initiate our own action, the basis of freedom is accounted for in theory. However, since Berkeley says there is no difference between willing and thinking, the consequence of this theory is that one is free to do whatever his thought suggests to him. Rather than freedom, this is more correctly called license. Without the limitations of the time and space dimension, freedom runs rampant. One is free even to live contradictions since a contradictory can be thought, even though it cannot be realized in action. So much freedom becomes a liability rather than an asset. Sartre, for example, is speaking as an idealist when he says that man carries the responsibility for the whole world on his shoulders. His freedom becomes a responsibility too great to bear. Every action that he takes makes its mark upon the rest of mankind. Traditional philosophy objects that such freedom belongs only to God. The action of a finite person is like a pebble thrown into a pond. It causes concentric rings of motion in the water that finally dissipate, leaving the water still again. When immaterialism credits the human person with excessive freedom, the responsibility for his actions becomes so great that, in Sartre's words, man is "condemned to be free."

In answer to so much responsibility the idealist chooses to forfeit his freedom. Such is the effect of the extreme idealism found in various cults and "isms" such as communism. Rather than make choices which may cause him anxiety and condemnation, the person gives up his freedom of thought and action to a higher authority which he accepts without question. He then identifies with the cult or "ism," taking on the party line and acting in strict adherence to the rules. In this way he fulfills his perfectionist goal by being an ideal member of the group. Formalism in religion is also often practiced as an attempt to overcome anxiety by performing, to the letter of the law, various dogmatic rules. The seemingly inexplicable actions of Nazi war criminals are an example of forfeiting one's own moral principles for those of a higher authority. If the higher authority is God, then one's judgment and action will be determined by love and follow natural laws of justice and observation of human rights. But if the authority is evil, it will attempt to enslave the person and the refusal to exercise one's judgment can have disastrous consequences such as in the Jonestown massacre. The prevalence of this tendency is surprisingly common, many persons following, not like blind sheep, but like self-blinding sheep.

The well-known experiment performed by Stanley Milgram of Yale University bears repeating since it demonstrates the tendency to sacrifice one's freedom to an authority in order to escape responsibility.[5] A wide sampling of subjects was invited to take part in the experiment. They were told that the purpose of the experiment was to discover whether or not punishment by electric shock would enhance learning, whereas the real purpose of the experiment was to test the degree of obedience to authority among persons of different backgrounds under ordinary circumstances. Each subject was allowed to draw a slip to decide whether he or she would be the learner or the teacher. However, all of the slips said "teacher" since the study was to find out whether the teacher would exercise passive or active obedience to the experimenter. The same learner took part each time the experiment was conducted, responding according to a set plan.

The learner was strapped in an electric chair. Subjects were told that an electrode was attached to the shock generator in the adjoining room. To improve credibility the experimenter said the shocks could be extremely painful to the learner but would be harmless. The teacher was then told to administer the test to the learner and, if he did not respond correctly, the teacher was to prod him with electric shocks of increasing intensity.

The immediate purpose of the experiment was to see how intense a shock each teacher would administer before he or she would refuse to follow the commands of the experimenter. The voltage and the response from the learner were roughly as follows:

			Extreme Intensity			*DANGER*	
Voltage	15	75	150	200	300	400	450
		moans	demands to be released		cannot stand pain	heart condition	no response

Dimensions of Freedom, Creativity, and Play 117

Psychologists predicted that the various teachers would refuse to continue when he or she realized that the learner was being harmed and that less than one tenth of a percent would administer the severest shock. Is this what actually happened?

In a typical case the teacher administered the test and the learner made an error. Pressing the button for 75 volts the teacher punished the learner who then let out a grunt. Since he continued to answer incorrectly, the teacher increased the voltage at which time the learner demanded to be released. At 180 volts the learner cried out with an agonized scream, "I can't stand the pain. Get me out of here." The teacher protested that he was killing the man but the experimenter told him whether the learner liked it or not he must complete the test. The teacher then followed with an extreme intensity shock of 300 volts and the learner screamed that his heart was bothering him. After 400 volts the learner was not heard from nor did his answers appear on the signal box. The experimenter told the teacher that, although the shocks were painful, he must go on to the end. After ensuring himself that the experimenter would assume all responsibility for the learner's welfare, the teacher administered the highest intensity of 450 volts marked extreme danger and continued to do so until stopped by the experimenter.

Although psychologists estimated less than 1%, over 50% of the teachers gave the learner the maximum shock! Whether or not the subjects administered severe shocks depended upon whether they exercised their own judgment or obeyed the authority of the experimenter. Milgram's conclusion is that ordinary people,

> without any particular hostility on their part, can become agents in a terrible destructive process. Moreover, even when the destructive effects of their work becomes patently clear, and they are asked to carry out actions incompatible with fundamental standards of morality, relatively few people have the resources needed to resist authority.[6]

The giving-over of authority to avoid responsibility of making decisions is made evident by the responses of the teachers. According to a *responsibility clock*, those who used their own judgment and resisted the experimenter saw "themselves as principally responsible for the suffering of the learner, assigning 48% responsibility to themselves and 39% to the experimenter."[7] Those who were obedient in administering the maximum voltage, assigned greater responsibility to the experimenter than to themselves and assigned twice as much blame to the learner! Although those who obeyed the authority did not derive any pleasure from their action, they took satisfaction in doing their job properly, a characteristic of idealism which places more credulity in perfectionism than in real life situations. Other teachers seemed to have been more influenced by a materialist fear of punishment "since they were totally convinced of the wrongness of what they were doing but could not bring themselves to make an open break with the authority." Loss of freedom is concomitant with the giving-over of responsibility. At this point immaterialism turns into its opposite, since materialism, too, has neither freedom nor responsibility.

The Dimension of Freedom According to Traditional Philosophy

Does *to be* for a human being mean *to be free*? If Being has any meaning for us at all, it will be because we, ourselves, actuate our own powers, making ourselves to be as we choose to be. This in no way denies the influences of heredity and environment but contends that we have the power to determine how we relate to Being. Traditional philosophy maintains that we possess immaterial will power by means of which we are empowered to act freely.

Will power, like intellectual power, is self-reflective. This is a simultaneous double action, not possible to a material power limited by time and space. With intellectual power, for example, we know that we know something or know that we don't know something. With will power, the self can perform the double action of willing to will or willing not to will, i.e., we can accept or reject whatever entices us. "The will wills that it will," says Aquinas.[8] This double action which requires a power that is immaterial is the basis of freedom. Without immateriality, a man could not be free.

How does our freedom function? We can choose to choose a good, thereby consenting to our choice, or choose to not choose a good, thereby dissenting to our choice. We can give consent to a good that appeals to us or we can dissent from it by substituting a less appetizing good that we value more. For example, we may strongly desire amusement but choose to complete our work because it leads to a greater end which we value more than our pleasure. Unlike an animal who has only a choice of means to an end not of his own choosing, since we originate our own ends, we have both the means and the end within our power. Realization of the various ends we choose is made possible by setting up a system of graduated values. We begin with those projects we are presently engaging in, and looking into the reason for our actions, find that they lead us to even greater ends. For example, we study because we wish to have a successful career. But the career is itself a means to a higher end, e.g., to become independent or to be helpful to others. In each step of these graduated values, the more comprehensive reason determines how we pursue the means to that end. If we desire a career merely for the purpose of earning money, we will study to make high grades in order to qualify for the best positions. But if we have a higher goal of wishing to help others, we will study with care in order to learn what can be of assistance to them. When we will to will or, in other words, consent to our own choice, the consent is determined by the values that we have chosen to actuate. If the means are consistent with the end desired and are morally good in themselves, we will approve the means. If a mean does not lead to the end desired, we will reject the mean although it may be in itself desirable.

All values finally lead to the good of which there is no greater. Anyone faced with a choice of a limited or an unlimited good will, by nature, choose the latter. It is only infinite Good, i.e. God, who can completely satisfy us, says Aquinas. Infinite Good is the apex of our value system, the supreme *value* upon which all other goods are *evaluated*.

The capacity to perceive a lattice of means to end is peculiar to intellectual power. It is only an immaterial power that can create a series of means to end relations, leading to a single over-all end. The biologist Goldstein says that setting up an overall means to end relation requires us

> to view a single experience within a larger context, i.e., to assume the "attitude toward the possible," to maintain freedom of decision regarding different possibilities. This attitude is peculiar to man ....[9]

Since we devise our own value system, our actions, too, are self-instigated. If we do not appreciate the value system we have set up, we can alter it. Although we do not always have *freedom from* environmental factors, as human beings we have freedom *to* and freedom *for.* Freedom gives us our own value system and the liberty to put it into effect or to change it.

According to Aristotle, all men desire the good and the good is their *to be.* To increase in being is the goal of every human being. This is accomplished by choosing those ends which more closely approach the apex of the value system. There is a hiatus between ego-related values and infinite Good. It is only by overcoming ego-centrism and caring for others that we can approach the ultimate Good. We cannot possess God but, through imitating him, we attain our highest good. Our attention becomes less and less centered upon our own pleasure as we become more capable of loving others. Ego-centrism changes into love of self and self-love into love of the other for his sake. As values expand to include others, there is an increment of being that rebounds to the self. To profit in this way is not an intentional choice on the part of the self but the by-product of our choice of the other and of infinite Being as our ultimate Good over our own ego-centric ends. An example is Viktor Frankl's experience in a Nazi concentration camp. Frankl had an opportunity to escape from the torture he was suffering but instead made the self-sacrificing choice of remaining with the typhus patients entrusted to his care. After having made his decision, he experienced an increase in his own being which gave him inward peace. By remaining, Frankl unintentionally saved his own life.

> As soon as I had told him with finality that I had made up my mind to stay with my patients, the unhappy feeling left me. I did not know what the following days would bring, but I had gained an inward peace that I had never experienced before.[10]

According to Aquinas, we address ourselves to the question of the good when, with our intellectual power in coaptation with our will power, we produce a *word of the heart*.[11] Rather than speculative knowledge, the word of the heart is a value judgment, effectuated by connatural knowledge or intuition. For example, Plato mentions that Socrates depended upon his *daimon* (intuition) to let him know when something should not be done. Whereas, for Socrates, intuition seemed to be more often a dissent from action than an impetus to act, there are positive intuitions informing us what is right to do. This may be an intuition rather than a logical imperative. The difficulty is to determine whether or not this is a valid criterion to follow. In most instances, we consider, not only the intuition, but an ethical decision as to whether an action should be committed.

Before we can choose those means which will successfully bring us to our chosen ends, we ask the question, *Are these adequate and justifiable means?* According to traditional philosophy, this question is answered by measuring the means by principles of justice. Actions are determined by the general principle: Good should be done and evil avoided. Since a good action is one that upholds justice and justice is based upon human rights, the major premise of a syllogism is a declaration of a human right. The minor premise of the syllogism is the circumstances that determine whether this is or is not an example of the major premise. And the conclusion is a judgment culminating in an actual act to carry out the means to this end or to forego it.

Major: Stealing is an unjust taking of another's property.

Minor: This property belongs to another person.

Conclusion: To take it would be an act of stealing.

Practical conclusion: Dissent to carry out this act.

This is a four-term practical syllogism rather than the speculative three-term syllogism. The conclusion does not necessarily follow the major premise since, even though we perceive the conclusion is that we should not steal, we can close off our reasoning process thereby allowing ourselves to commit the act. Although the major premise is formulated by a study of ethical principles, the practical conclusion is a free choice of whether or not we wish to act according to the maxim: Good should be done and evil avoided. Lack of information about the circumstances resulting in an unintentional unjust act is not blameworthy, e.g., if we cannot arrive at a correct conclusion to the syllogism because of lack of information. Other than this, the responsibility for a decision rests upon our own intention.

Traditional philosophy has been criticized for overemphasizing the moral law without sufficient consideration of human fallibility or the changing aspects of morality. Although it remains basically the same, morality, just as law, is being reformulated as fast as history proceeds, says James.

How are we able to choose a lesser good in opposition to our value system? The self can use its will power to take command over its intellectual power. We then produce a false statement, e.g., by closing our mind to the greater good the lesser good will appear to be a true good. For example, if the greater good is honesty and the lesser good is acquiring money, we can ignore honesty, and money then becomes the good. This often is accompanied by rationalization, e.g., I will submit a larger claim to my insurance company than my damages warrant because the money means more to me than it does to a large company. However, since the proper end of intellectual power is to seek truth, when we release our intellectual power, we will once again be aware that it is better to be honest than to falsify a claim. At that time we will suffer what is known as a guilty conscience. This should not be confused with the guilty conscience spoken of by Freud and other exponents of a materialist theory of being. We are not offending the internalized norms of parents and society but the value system which we, ourselves, choose as leading us to infinite Good. If this is repeated too often, rationalization will become a habit and the value system by which freedom is maintained will be forfeited. Losing our self-determination, we will then be reduced to satisfying our passions.

Traditional philosophy maintains that for the most part our senses are under the control of our power of will. With will power we rule our senses with a "politic sovereignty," according to Aquinas. The immaterialist, on the other hand, considers the senses as a lower form of being. Pascal, for example, wore a hair shirt under his coat to prick his senses into servility and sprinkled gall over his food to deprive his palate of pleasant sensations. This parallels the severe discipline sometimes advocated for unruly children. A more realistic approach is to realize that if you use a "politic sovereignty" with your senses or your children they won't become unruly in the first place. At times our sense appetite dominates our will, e.g., when we are tired or ill, which reminds us that we are virtually (though not actually) animal, just as extreme thirst reminds us that we are virtually chemical. But, for traditional philosophy, if our sense appetite does not act in our best interest, it is because we let it deviate from our value system.

The inability to control our habits is very often due to the way we form our world-model. If we fail to enrich our world-model with sufficient possibilities, the error of materialism, we will try to overcome the consequent boredom by pursuing material pleasures. This dissipation of our time does not rectify our lack of interest but increases boredom. Unless one takes one's destiny in hand, the condition will become more aggravated.

If we lean toward immaterialism we will find that the opposite problem is ours, i.e., we form our world with contradictory possibilities. If we pressure ourselves to do our work with consistent perfection, we may find that we cannot achieve such a goal and then look for a scapegoat to cover our failures. If a bad habit is due to depression or nervousness, we should examine our value system. Have we chosen a career that is particularly suited for us? Does it place undue stress upon us? The standards that we set for ourselves must be consistent with the limitations of time and space with which we all must cope. We should have high aspirations but be careful to form a realistic world-model, undertaking challenging projects, but leaving aside those which we find cause us undue stress. We can allay depression by realizing that we are all limited beings.

According to the psychologist Carl Jung, if we are not aware of our limitations, we repress our errors and our evils into our personal unconscious. Without realizing we do so, we then project them upon a scapegoat. The human race has a long history of scapegoatism. Frazier mentions numerous instances of scapegoatism occurring, not only in primitive societies but also at the present time. At first the practice was employed to rid a tribe of pestilences, for there was at that time an equation between evil and sickness. The sickness was transferred to a vessel which was sent downstream to infect another village. The practice was later expanded to include moral evils and the scapegoat generally was an animal. Still later, human beings often played the role of scapegoat. In Greece, for example, some unfortunate outcast was first given dried figs, a barley loaf, and cheese (reminding one of the banquet served to criminals before their execution), then he was beaten while flutes played a symbolic tune. Afterwards he was burned on a pyre built of the wood of forest trees, and his ashes were cast into the sea.[12] The people believed that their sins were cast away with the scapegoat. The New Year brought forth resolutions for a new beginning.

Scapegoatism is continuing now on a personal level rather than as a social custom. We repress our shortcomings letting others take the blame. But by not admitting our guilt we repeat our errors over and over, such as a person who is perpetually tardy. We can only integrate ourself if we withdraw our projections and accept our own weaknesses and errors. The attempt to allay a guilty conscience by the use of scapegoats results in a loss of self. The person without a shadow is a flat personality, according to Jung. By accepting our own failings we can more easily accept the failings of others, realizing that perfection does not belong to finiteness. Unless we consider ourselves superior to the human race, since we all make mistakes and commit evil, it should not be too difficult to admit our limitations.

Christianity introduced a different kind of scapegoatism. Jesus, as the Paschal lamb, willingly takes on our burden of guilt but only on the condition that we recognize our own evil and ask for forgiveness. By his sacrifice on the cross, Jesus paid for our sins. By believing on him, we are redeemed to eternal life.

The Dimension of Freedom
According to Contemporary Philosophy

Contemporary philosophy objects to an association of conscience with evil. Traditional philosophy, for example, interprets evil as a privation of being that *ought* to be. It tells loudly about *making mistakes* or doing evil, of what *ought* to be rather than what *can* be. Heidegger believes that, whereas this is a satifactory definition of the non-being of the present-at-hand, it is not appropriately applied to Dasein. The idea of guilt must "be detached from relationship to law or *ought* such that by failing to comply with it one loads himself with guilt." We should be careful not to have too narrow a concept of freedom so that it becomes merely deliberate choice. The notion of conscience, as the satisfying of manipulable rules and public norms, and guilt, as the failure to satisfy them, is too superficial and impersonal for contemporary philosophy. Conscience in its affirmative role is a personal call to pro-ject oneself into the future by coming to a realization of the possible role he or she may play in the world community. According to Heidegger,

> Being-guilty does not first result from an indebtedness, but that, on the contrary, indebtedness becomes possible only *on the basis* of a primordial Being-guilty."[13]

This primordial Being-guilty is not interpreted as *guilt* as in traditional philosophy. Rather Dasein is its own null basis of being in the sense that it is *not yet* but must fulfill itself. For Heidegger, conscience is primordial, underlying any concrete acts. He interprets being-guilty as wanting to have a conscience so that we can be answerable to our potentiality for being. Rather than looking for relief from conscience, as in traditional philosophy, we are *called* by conscience to fulfill ourselves. In order to concentrate our energies on developing our possibilities, it is necessary that we have a positive notion of Dasein as *being there*, i.e., as being available to Being. The call of conscience beckons us to that which we can be. It is a call to respond to the possibilities of one's being, i.e., to live authentically.

The call of conscience implies tension as a necessary consequence of the numerous possibilities that are open to us and our inability to effectuate all of them in the space/time continuum. Sadler notes:

> We must be wary of seeking peace within conscience. The search for an easy and quiet conscience is not necessarily a longing for the fullness of life but may really be for death.[14]

We can realize our destiny only in relation to others, which necessarily means to live authentically, we must struggle to find our place in Dasein's controversial ways of formulating world. By sharing cultures, the people of all nations can begin to overcome their isolation.

It is by means of anxiety that we first become aware of our inauthenticity. Anxiety is to be distinguished from fear which is caused by a known object from which we flee. Anxiety, on the other hand, has no known object but is a shrinking back from our own inauthenticity and loss of self. We may involve ourselves in busyness to avoid the anxiety we experience in turning away from ourselves, but such busyness is intermittently interrupted by a *hollow* feeling that questions, "Is this all there is to life?" When we fail to hear the call of conscience, we feel the encroachment of non-being.

We respond to the call of conscience through courage, says Tillich.

> Courage always includes a risk, it is always threatened by non-being, whether the risk of losing oneself and becoming a thing within the whole of things or of losing one's world in an empty self-relatedness. Courage needs the power of being, a power transcending the non-being...which is present in the anxiety of emptiness and meaninglessness.[15]

The call of conscience summons us to respond to the many dimensions of our being. We have many different possibilities vying for expression and the choices we make leave others undone. We need to select carefully so that our world-model is a congruous whole without contradictions. Sadler notes that authentic conscience is "marked by the phenomenon of the convergence of different possibilities." He compares this to music:

> The full sound of authentic conscience is not a single tone, certainly not a lullaby, but a harmoniously structured melody where divergent tones which exist in tension with others nevertheless interpenetrate to form an exciting, integral whole, moving us to respond with our whole existence toward achieving our truth, our real identities.[16]

It is in creativity that contemporary philosophy seeks the dimension of freedom. Freedom is not something to be taken for granted. It grows out of the resourcefulness of the human spirit. Viktor Frankl points out the differences in ability among prisoners in a Nazi concentration camp to withstand the devastating conditions of the camp which utterly curtailed their freedom. If the prisoner's world-model was centered upon solicitude for others, even in the worst of conditions, there was always something for him to think about and to hope for. "He who has a *why* to live for can bear with almost any *how*." Frankl comes to the conclusion that it is our capacity to find meaning in our lives that sustains us in freedom. "It is this spiritual freedom - which cannot be taken away - that makes life meaningful and purposeful."[17] Unless we multiply our needs by an insatiable desire for material goods, we are given bountiful resources to satisfy more than our own needs. To concentrate our attention on our own selfish interests is like a dog chasing his own tail. It is only by transcending our egoism that we can experience spiritual freedom.

Freedom entails the responsibility of each citizen to realize whatever potential he may have to help tip the balance in favor of peace and brotherhood among all men. We can no longer afford to give up our freedom of decision but must do our own thinking and exercise our own freedom in the interests of a world community if we expect to overcome the hostility of warfare. The citizens of all nations will need to join forces to create a world community of persons if we are to have peace in the world. We must act in freedom, not determined by our own interests, but seeking justice for all. The other side of the coin of freedom is responsibility - responsibility not just to ourselves but to as many others as we have the capacity to assist. It is becoming increasingly apparent that we do not live merely in a country but in a world community. We stand or fall with the entire human race. With starvation and disease rampant in the world, nothing less than employing the full extent of our powers will bring about the needed alleviation of suffering. To do so is to live authentically. The possibilities of each being are novel and unique. We do not need to rely upon the *they* to form our opinions for us nor should we feel obliged to conform to the habitual. We live authentically when we exercise our own initiative and creativity, fulfilling our destiny as a being-in-the-world-with-others.

The Dimension of Creativity

We discover our freedom in the creative act. Unlike Freudian sublimation which originates in personal repressed content, creativity is an expression of the fullness of Being. The artist's intuition transcends the personal. His work is a projection into the future and so lacks conformity with the *they* of publicness, which is the death of innovation. According to Rollo May, this requires courage. "If it were possible to control the artist, and I don't believe it is - it would mean the death of art."[18] Creative effort is not merely sublimation of the repressed content of the id but is an expression of the voice of Being.

The creative act is an encounter between the self and non-being in which non-being is overcome. A Chinese poet defines the creative act: "We poets struggle with non-being to force it to yield being. We knock upon silence for an answering music." To create is to witness and record the triumph of being over non-being. What was not has come-to-be.

Creativity engages the whole person, our conscious, preconscious, and unconscious, says Rollo May.

> For the creative impulse is the speaking of the voice and the expressing of the forms of the preconscious and unconscious; and this is by its very nature, a threat to rationality and external control.[19]

Our inspirations come from our collective unconscious, according to Jung, which is the inheritance we have received from our primitive forefathers. The contents of our collective unconscious are in the form of archetypes, i.e., ideal figures such as Venus who rises from the sea (the symbol of the unconscious). The archetypes are universal and are participated in by all races. Each archetype has both a positive side and a negative side, the latter representing the evil qualities of mankind, e.g., a witch as opposed to the beauty of the *anima*. Such opposites depict the contest between good and evil. According to Jung, myths and fairy tales reveal this common inheritance, e.g., sleeping beauty is a symbol of the male unconscious *anima* which is awakened when the conscious male ego integrates the self. When poets call upon their muse, they are soliciting an inspiration from the "charmed circle" of their collective unconscious.

A particular relation to Being is revealed in the created work. Because it is to society that he holds a mirror, this does not mean the artist subscribes to the philosophy he unconsciously depicts. The artwork may not only manifest the present but predict the future. Although there are many variations within each, there emerges characteristic kinds of art corresponding to the different notions of Being held by the various philosophies.

That immaterialism misses the relation of art to Being is illustrated by Plato. Since it is only in the heaven of universal Forms that reality is to be discovered, Platonic Idealism denigrates human creativity. Artwork is twice removed from the pure forms; since the artifact is already a copy of the Forms, the artist's work in portraying the artifact is merely a copy of a copy. Plato objects that because of its appeal, the artwork deceives the spectator into believing the copy is really true. Although artistic creations are enticing, e.g., Homer inspires awe and love, artwork is inferior because it appeals to the emotions rather than to the rational principle in the soul.[20] But what Plato overlooked is that the artwork does not simply imitate particulars in time and space but expresses those universal ideas found in the particular. The artist of his time was imbued, although unconsciously, with the same ideas that Plato himself held. The artwork was made to resemble as closely as possible the perfection and beauty of the pure Forms. In Greek statuary, for example, individual flaws were erased in favor of the perfection of the universal. "Phidias when carving Jupiter, did not copy anything real but kept his looks fixed upon "*species pulcritudinis eximia quaedam*, which he had in his soul and which directed his art and his hand."[21] Just as the universal is emphasized in idealism, correct proportion is characteristic of this art since the universal reveals itself through what is common and alike rather than what is individual and different. It is said that Zeuxis took the best of five Crotonian maidens in order to paint his Helen.[22] Idealism persists in both philosophy and art, placing its emphasis upon universal perfection rather than upon the singular with its eccentricities.

In traditional aesthetics, as in its conception of truth, there is emphasis upon the universal portrayed in the particular. The artist, for example, captures and crystallizes in paint or other media a particular scene which is a symbol of the universal character of being, such as the wonder of nature or the humility of the bent figure of a workman. Traditional art, like its ethics, follows formal rules to guide the artist in the proper use of materials, correct perspective, and so forth. Aquinas notes that the beautiful work of art should have the qualities of harmony, proportion, and clarity. The over-all criterion by which the artwork is judged is its ability to portray in truth and beauty the universal reality that it engenders. A superior painting or other work of art reveals a spiritual dimension and even a mundane scene is presented in such a way as to portray universal qualities present in the particular. According to Tolstoy, the more the artwork relates to the common man, the more aesthetic it is. Appreciation for this art requires that the spectator enter into the artwork as if he were present to the reality it depicts.

If matter takes precedence over mind, as in materialism, the artwork will be nothing more than a cutting from the material environment, enhanced by increased size and so forth. Such, for example, is Robert Rauschenberg's (accidental) dirt paintings; Andy Warhol's stacked soup cans; Carl Andre's *grave site*, a tiny pile of sand made by *dumping* and *pouring*; and Marcel Duchamp's *Fountain*, actually an urinal. It is selected on the basis of its timeliness as an expression of the environment. Materialism has no criteria by which to judge the aesthetic value of the artwork. In his *Of the Standard of Taste*, Hume says, "We seek in vain for a standard by which we can reconcile the contrary of sentiment."[23] Why, for example, is the tie Picasso painted blue chosen over the child's tie painted blue? Since its theory of knowledge is relative, materialism must depend upon other art criticism with which the reputation of the artist is established.

Since materialism moves in only one direction - away from meaning toward the purely physical, such is the nature of the movement called *meaningless work*. This art shuns any worthy end, i.e., work that accomplishes a conventional purpose. An example of this art form is transferring wooden blocks from one box to another and then returning them to the original box. Whereas prior art forms were intended to communicate meaning and therefore had social significance, this *art* form rejects any purpose or value. It is an attempt to express meaninglessness or futility. The human person does not transcend himself to overcome non-being but merely rebels against convention. Just as the actions of the adolescent child do not suggest a way of life but merely reflect rebellion against parental influence, so this *art* form rejects all that history offers us in the way of culture. Since it does not overcome non-being, it leads to the death of art. But since it is the nature of man to transcend himself in his openness to Being, creativity continues in spite of non-art's efforts to seek to return all to the elements.

Contemporary philosophy overcomes the mind/matter dichotomy to realize a synthesis in which creator and creating work cooperate. Heidegger objects to the idea that a work of art should merely depict an actually existing thing successfully. "Is it our opinion," asks Heidegger, "that the painting draws a likeness from something actual and transposes it into a product of artistic production? By no means."[24] Being freed from the formalism of traditional art, the artist is able to exercise freedom in his creativity. The artwork is not considered to be a portrayal of a *thing* but a disclosure of Being. The artwork clears and illuminates Being.

Art is truth setting itself to work. All self-initiated products are works of art insofar as they set forth truth. The artwork is both determined by the idea and, in turn, determines the idea. Creativity thus overcomes the art of everydayness typical of materialism and the absolutism of the universal typical of immaterialism. The created work opens up a world and sustains it abidingly.

> By the opening up of a world, all things gain their lingering and hastening, their remoteness and nearness, their scope and limits.... A work by being a work, makes room for that spaciousness.[25]

The artwork is set forth by striving. It is a striving between towering and repose. Towering is the worlding of world and repose is earth insofar as it is "that on which and in which man bases his dwelling," i.e., his native ground. As we paint colors onto the canvas, the potential towering of world shines through the medium and the medium reposes this by telling us what is possible in the way of communication and what will not work. It is by listening to the silent voice of Being that we reconcile the opposites of towering and repose in the artwork. We point up, deepen, spread out, and focus that which the canvas or clay offers us, intensifying potential towering and letting actual repose take over in a coincidence of opposites. *The artwork opens up the Being of beings*, closing the hiatus between ourselves and Being. As we commune with Being through the medium of the work, Being illuminates the artwork. It is by depicting this illumination that the artist's work creates for humanity a clearing where it can feel the presence of Being.

The Dimension of Play

It is not only creative work that overcomes non-being but also creative play. In fact, Schiller goes so far as to say that man is only fully a man when he plays. In the traditional mode of defining essences, play is known by contrasting it to work; work is labor or effort motivated toward a specific end, whereas play is for amusement. However, this definition does not take into account the essential role that play plays in the unfolding of our being.

According to Piaget, it is in play that language is originated. In his intensive studies of children, Piaget notes that the child first learns to play when he is attracted by the functioning of an object in his environment. He cites the case of Jacqueline who accidentally set an orange peel rocking back and forth. This became a ritual as, looking first at its convex side, she set the peel rocking.[26] Animals, too, engage in ritual play. However, the child advances to imaginary play, deliberately acting out a meaningful relationship. The gestures used in imaginative play eventually become symbolized. This is the beginning of language. The language of a child is intimate, belonging to him alone, since it is only he who knows the meaning of the symbols of his private world. Only later does he learn a common language. Phillips notes that Piaget corrects the poet Wordsworth's definition of language.

> Wordsworth expressed beautifully (as poets are wont to do) one point of view on the relation of language to thinking: "the word," he said, "is not the dress of thought, but its very incarnation." "Not so," says Piaget. "Language is the vehicle by which thought is socialized and thus made logical, but it

is not the original basis of, nor does it ever become the whole of human thinking."[27]

Since language grows out of the internalized symbols of imaginary play, play performs a vital role in the evolution of speech. Ricoeur agrees with Piaget that we cannot consider language apart from the lived experience that originated it. "If we detach the living experience from the symbol, we take away from the experience that which completes its meaning."[28] We cannot, therefore, consider the abstract concept as the foundation of language. Rather language grows out of the early experience of man in myth, which is the narration of the acting out of his world-model in play.

The dimension of play includes the spiritual as well as the mundane. Ricoeur notes that myth depicts man's transcendence in-the-world toward that which is unknown in experience. Materialism cannot explain language since it accounts merely for the things of the environment whereas the myth aims at Being-in-totality, that which is unknown because it is not yet experienced by man. Ricoeur says: "Hence, the myth has the function of guarding the finite contours of the signs which, in their turn, refer to the plenitude that man aims at rather than experiences."[29] Play opens up the possibility of dimensions not yet experienced and so charts a unique direction for the self through the medium of symbols. Huizinga notes that poetry and music were born and nourished in play. Play is not what is done but the spirit with which it is done. Any action based on possibility rather than actuality takes the form of play. He states that "real civilization cannot exist in the absence of a certain play element, for civilization presupposes limitation and mastery of the self...."[30] Mastery of the self is never direct but comes about by *playing out* numerous possibilities and then limiting ourselves to those which prove to be the most rewarding to ourselves and others.

Work and play are a coincidence of opposites which constitutes creativity. Work without play becomes unimaginative drudgery; whereas play without work is non-communicative imagination. Although our inspirations appear to originate in our unconscious, the richer our conscious life, the more productive will be our unconscious inspirations. Whereas we cannot will creativity's intuitions, we can will "to give ourselves to the encounter with intensity of dedication and commitment," says Rollo May. Anything less than commitment will not triumph. Creativity does not occur as a *Bacchic letting go*. The creative vision must be accompanied by periods of sustained work. Describing his creative work, Ingmar Bergman says: "I throw a spear into the darkness. That is intuition. Then I must send an army into the darkness to find the spear. That is intellect." The magic is replaced by hard work.

The creativity of work and play is not merely avocation but vocation. Our destiny is a work of art which we, the artists, create as Being silently speaks to us, directing us to what is possible and true and accomplishing in us the fulfillment of our being. Bragdon asserts that the important thing in the practice of any art is not what the practitioner is able to produce, but what *it* (Being) is able to produce in him.

> Through art the life-force achieves its most eloquent utterance: outlines most clearly those archetypal images to which it is ever striving to give form and movement on the lighted stage of the world.... The artist's opportunity is great and his tasks arduous to the extent that he lends himself to this activity of the life-force.[31]

It is not the final product that determines whether or not we live aesthetically. Rather, *the animating spirit whereby a thing gets itself done determines its true quality and spirit*. This animating spirit is manifested in love.

Summary on Freedom

Materialism

> Presupposition: Man acts mechanically or by instinct (stimulus/response)
>
> Question: If man acts by stimulus/response, is he free?
>
> Conclusion: Because man must respond to whatever stimulates him the most as the time, he is not free.

Immaterialism

>Presupposition: Man can do whatever he can think.

>Question: What effect does this have on freedom?

>Conclusion: License entails so much responsibility, it is given away to an authority with consequent loss of freedom.

Traditional Philosophy

>Presupposition: The human person acts rationally (with powers of intellect and will).

>Question: How does reason help the human person to be free?

>Conclusion: With will power he consents or dissents to choose on the basis of his value system leading to infinite Good.

Contemporary Philosophy

>Presupposition: Lived experience discovers the belonging together of Dasein and Being.

>Question: How can I realize my freedom?

>Conclusion: By listening to the call of conscience I realize my freedom as a projection toward Being exercised through my creativity.

1. Rollo May, *Psychology and the Human Dilemma* (New York: D. Van Nostrand, 1967), pp. 161-167, by permission of Brooks/Cole Publishing Co.

2. Sigmund Freud, *The Ego and the Id*, trans. J. Riviere, ed. J. Strachey (New York: W. W. Norton, 1960), p. 15

3. "Behavior Mod Behind the Walls, Use on Prisoners," *Time Magazine* (March 11, 1974), p. 74

4. Ibid.

5. Stanley Milgram, *Obedience to Authority* (New York: Harper & Row, 1969) also (London: Tavistock Publications, Ltd.)

6. Ibid., p. 6

7. Ibid., p. 203

8. Thomas Aquinas, *De Ver.* 22, 12

9. Goldstein, *Human Nature*, p. 113

10. Viktor Frankl, *Man's Search for Meaning*, trans. I. Lasch (New York: Simon & Schuster, 1959), p. 58

11. For a more complete treatment of this subject see E. Ecker Steger, "Verbum Cordis," *Divus Thomas* (Piacenza: Colegio Alberoni, 1978), vol. 81 #16

12. Sir James Frazier, *The New Golden Bough*, ed. T. H. Gautier (New York: Criterion Books, 1959), p. 541

13. Heidegger, *Being and Time*, p. 328

14. William A. Sadler, *Existence and Love* (New York: Charles Scribner, 1969), p. 232

15. Paul Tillich, *The Courage to Be*, (New Haven: Yale University Press, 1952), p. 152

16. Sadler, *Existence* ..., p. 232

17. Frankl, *Man's Search* ..., p. 66

18. Rollo May, *The Courage to Create* (New York: W. W. Norton, 1976), p. 85

19. Ibid., pp. 84-85

20. Plato, *Republic*, X

21. *Orator ad Brutum*, Ch.II

22. Benedetto Croce, *Aesthetic*, trans. Douglas Ainislie (New York: The Noonday Press, 1956), p. 171

23. Stephen David Ross, ed., *An Anthology of Aesthetic Theory* (Albany: State University of New York, 1984), p. 94

24. Martin Heidegger, *Poetry, Language, Thought*, trans. A. Hofstader (New York: Harper & Row, 1975), p. 37

25. Ibid., p. 45

26. Phillips, Jr. *Origins of Intellect*, p. 45

27. Ibid., p. 59

28. Paul Ricoeur, *The Symbolism of Evil*, trans. E. Buchanan, (Boston: Beacon Press, 1969), p. 171

29. Ibid., p. 169

30. Johan Huizinga, *Homo Ludens* (Boston: Beacon Press, 1950), p. 28

31. Claude Bragdon, *The Eternal Poles* (New York: Alfred A. Knopf, 1931), p. 71

Chapter VI

THE DIMENSION OF LOVE

Love is elusive, defying analysis. However, to ignore the question of love because it is enigmatic would be to reduce philosophical wisdom to mere science. Lived experience reveals that love is as varied as the persons who love. Just as materialism and immaterialism represents the extremities of possible philosophies, so their notion of love is at opposite ends of the pole. The materialist sees love as the pursuit of pleasure whereas the immaterialist perceives it as the pursuit of a universal ideal. Traditional philosophy is more objective, defining the basic structure of love. But love is made more visible by contemporary philosophy, whose method is phenomenological inquiry into love as lived experience.

Love is a unifying experience, taking within itself a number of opposites which, when reconciled, cause an expansion of our being. The first question to be investigated concerning love is: Does the notion of love as espoused by materialism and by immaterialism offer us a reconciliation of the contraries inherent in love?

Love as Instinct
According to Materialism

Since its presupposition is that the human being is nothing more than a sensing being, what is the meaning of love, according to materialism? To equate human beings and animals means that love can be nothing more than a response to instinctive demands. Since there is no difference between inanimate objects and human persons, *love* is reduced to *like*. We like the one who gives us pleasure and reject whoever gives us pain. Hume states, "It is from the prospect of pain or pleasure that the aversion or propensity arises towards any object." For Freud, also, since the id or unconscious is the pleasure principle, we are necessitated to choose the material good that most satisfies our appetite for pleasure. Once the ego appeases the appetite by cathecting (dissipating) energy upon the object, there is no further need for the object and the love then ceases. Martin Buber calls this an I-It relation since a good is loved merely for its usefulness. Although it is the perfective qualities of an object that serve our needs, e.g., we like a peach that is ripe but not rotten, can such utilitarianism be called love if applied to a human person? To add up the good qualities of a person just as one would inspect a peach, would appear to reduce man to less than human. Buber answers this question by stating that the I-It relation of materialism is necessary for living in the time and space dimension, "but he who lives with It alone is not a man."[1]

For materialism, eros is reduced to the physical manifestation of love. Since our sexual nature, for example, is equated with that of an animal, its purpose is entirely physical, e.g., to propagate or to nurture, rather than to express love. According to Rollo May, sex thus alienated from love becomes a mischievous plaything. Emphasis upon the technical aspects of the sex act fosters sexual impotence. The technically efficient lover "has lost the power to be carried away; he knows only too well what he is doing. At this point, technology diminishes consciousness and demolishes eros."[2] A Don Juan, incapable of feeling the deep and lasting emotion of love, compensates by taking pride in his sexual achievements. Sex without love results in a loss of identity. Rollo May notes that the fig leaf once covering the genitals is, in this age, raised to hide the face. Rather than sharing the dignity that belongs to them as human beings, children exposed to sex scenes in the media, begin to see themselves as objects to be utilized. Rollo May notes that "the cult of technique destroys feelings, undermines passion, blots out individual identity."[3] Such license forgets that safeguarding children from illicit sexual media is a necessary condition to fostering a sense of human dignity. Illicit sex encourages rape and bestial behavior.

Is altruism possible in a materialist environment? For Hume, animals have a *natural propensity* to exhibit kindness and *benevolence*. Such benevolence has been demonstrated by Rhesus monkeys. In one experiment, a double compartment was set up with a glass divider so that a monkey in the first compartment could see and hear another monkey in the second compartment. When the first monkey pressed a lever, he was rewarded with food. After he had sufficiently associated the lever with the reward, it was re-wired so that, in addition to the food, it administered a shock to the monkey in the second compartment. Rather than hear the cry of pain from the other monkey, the first monkey starved himself to death. All of the monkeys except one, when given the same circumstances, sacrificed their lives rather than hear the sign of distress from the other monkey. If animals exercise benevolence, says Hume, it should be undeniable that human beings also have such a natural propensity. There are two questions to be raised concerning Hume's statement. Is it undeniable that, because an animal possesses certain powers, a man must also possess such powers? Secondly, should the actions of human beings be equated with the *natural propensities* of animals, e.g. does a human being, like an animal, always act spontaneously to a stimulus or is the human act of benevolence freely chosen? Materialism not only reduces love to its physical manifestation but contends that human altruism is just another form of instinctive gratification.

Freud emphasizes the important role of opposites such as the love/hate, life/death instincts. But, since his materialist view is patterned after the physical motions found in nature in which one contrary cannot exist simultaneously with another, e.g., a mountain cannot be erupting and inactive simultaneously, a reconciliation of the love/hate opposites is impossible. Freud uses the analogy of the female spider to explain the ambivalence of the love/hate or life/death instincts. After copulating with the male spider she catches in her web, the female spider then proceeds to consume the male. Freud thus hypostatizes hate, placing it on a par with love as a motivating force. Whereas spiritual love may include hate within itself (one loves this person but hates his destructive habits), materialism reduces love and hate to irreconcilable organic functions.

In summary, for materialism, love has no meaning other than an instinctive response to a stimulus which must be satisfied either for pleasure or for the useful good. After the need is satisfied, love ceases.

The Idealization of Love
According to Immaterialism

Immaterialism, representing the opposite extreme, also fails to reconcile contraries. Its notion of love denigrates the personal in favor of the universal. According to Plato, since men are involuntarily attracted to the sight of a beautiful body, love begins as the earthly irrational passion. The goddess of love Aphrodite, according to Greek literature, is unconquerable, destructive, and inescapable. She drives men mad and destroys their reason. In Sophocles' *Antigone*, the chorus chants:

> Love unconquered in fight,.... Who has you within him is mad. You twist the minds of the just. Wrong they pursue and are ruined .... For there is the goddess at play with whom no man can fight.[4]

Love was thought to be a universal force that enslaves the lover. It thus took on a compulsive note which belies the true essence of love.

According to Plato, this inferior form of love can be overcome through intellectual pursuits (the heavenly Aphrodite) which inspire an ecstatic flight to the intelligible forms. But personal love then becomes nothing more than a stepping stone to the higher achievement of attaining universal beauty.

> The loved thing is only an accident and a stimulus to the attainment of a content in which there is no need for this being to remain, where he is even out of place, for his palpable presence might disturb the ecstasy.[5]

The equation of the good with the beauty of the forms gave precedence to man's intellect over his will and idealized universal truth at the expense of human love. Gould notes that "Plato steers us toward a conception of love as a general - indeed a universal - phenomenon." However, the contraries of individual and universal good must be reconciled in order that love embody the full dimension of the human person. When the personal is sacrificed for the universal, love becomes a solitary flight without concern for the other for his sake. Guitton states:

> It can be said of Plato that he has wholly comprehended and justified everything, except love.... And that without doubt is why the spouse is never mentioned.[6]

Since personal love is denigrated, the value of family life is undermined. Rational creation rather than procreation is the way to immortality, according to Plato, who asks, "Who would not prefer the offspring of Hesiod to the children of physical desire?"[7] It is characteristic of immaterialism that the universal is over-valued at the expense of the personal. An example of the depersonalization of love is the Reverend Moon's wedding ceremony in which several thousand couples, mated by Moon or his attendants, were lined up and married in a communal wedding ceremony. Most of the brides were unacquainted with the groom chosen for them and many did not speak the same language. The vow they took was to the universal church rather than to the spouse.

This same lack of freedom is manifested in the romantic love of the middle ages in which the lack of conscious choice is symbolized by the idea expressed by the love potion. Jung explains romantic love as the phenomenon of the collective unconscious - the numinous archetypes of *anima* and *animus* at play. The male unconscious or *anima* falls in love with the female unconscious or *animus*. Such a love affair cannot be consummated in the everydayness of conscious life. Death is the only alternative. The romantic tale of Romeo and Juliet, for example, is a love story of *anima* and *animus*. Since they are universal personifications of the collective unconscious, they lack the personal note characteristic of conscious love.

The romantic love of the middle ages is the prototype of present day romance. Jung believed all love between the sexes has its basis in romantic love. Such love, however, must be brought to fruition as a coincidence of universal and personal, of unconscious and conscious, of ideal and real before it can have the freedom characteristic of true love.[8] It is the projection of the archetypal *anima* or *animus* upon a real person that is the root of romantic love. The collective archetype that complements the male ego is the *anima*. She is the prototype of creativity known to the poet as his muse. As the source of inspiration, she holds him captive to her beauty and charm. The unconscious archetype of the female ego is the *animus*. He is characterized by rationality, concern for worldly affairs, and heroism. When a man falls in love, it is with a woman upon whom he has projected his *anima*. He is enticed by his own unconscious but thinks it is the real woman whom he loves. The woman projects her unconscious *animus* upon a man who, because he matches the woman's unconscious, carries the personification well. This is love at first sight. But no person can match the perfection of the unconscious *anima* or *animus*. The lover must learn to accept his partner, not as his unconscious half, but for his or her sake, i.e., I-Thou relation. The lover will then appreciate the real person in her or his uniqueness rather than mistaking her or him for the unconscious archetype. And for love to endure, there must be a conscious decision to accept the real person. Rather than a *love potion*, real love requires the free consent of the lover.

According to Jung, marriage involves four rather than two, i.e., the male and the female egos and the *anima* and the *animus*. If the husband and wife undergo a self-transformation process, the collective unconscious projections are to a degree withdrawn and integrated with their own egos. The self comes into being as the coincidence of unconscious and conscious. The marriage then becomes compatible and productive. With the coincidence of these opposites, the husband and wife are able to share common interests and enjoy a mutual relationship.

According to Jung, if the unconscious is not integrated, the *anima* and the *animus* will continue to exercise their influence but in a negative manner by taking over the ego. In this event, the husband will appear to be very effeminate and the wife, on the other hand, will appear to be domineering and stubborn. Since this is not a conscious choice, neither will understand why he acts the way he does nor will he be able to control the outburst of his collective unconscious. To be motivated entirely by the ego leaves one vulnerable to the projections of the collective unconscious archetypes. But if the self-integration process occurs, conscious and unconscious are in coincidence and romantic love becomes true love.

Although Jung is able to reconcile the opposites of conscious and unconscious, he leaves us with the question: Are all men characterized by rational consciousness and a creative unconscious and, vice versa, do all women possess the opposite combination? In testing this, we find that it is certainly not universally true that men are consciously more intellectual. In fact, many more men claimed to have a creative conscious rather than a creative unconscious which Jung considered to be characteristic of women. Evidence does support the bipolar nature of the human person, however, the unconscious complementing those characteristics which are predominantly conscious or, it could be said, the right hemisphere complementing the left hemisphere of the brain.

It is also found that contemporary partners prefer to become friends before falling in love. This enhances freedom of choice, rather than relying upon the unconscious to take the first step in deciding who the most compatible partner would be.

Love of the Good
According to Traditional Philosophy

Under the influence of Judaeo-Christian thought, love lost its abstract universal character and became personified in the one God who is infinite Love. This placed emphasis upon power of will rather than of intellect as that by which man moves toward his ultimate end, the love of God. According to Nicholas de Cusa, God is the coincidence of the *explicatio* (unfolding) and the *complicatio* (enfolding) of all beings. It is from Love Itself that all acts of finite love unfold and to which they return.

According to Judaism, since God created man and woman in his own image, all persons are endowed with will and are free to love. Platonic love stressed the idea, the more perfect the object loved, the more perfect the love. However, the Christian message emphasizes the necessity of loving all persons and especially the poor, the sinner, the enemy, and the innocent. To love those in need is to love God. Sacrifice and penitence were incorporated into the notion of love. Although a misinterpretation of the Christian message, the centrifugal motion of love called *agape* was accepted as the ideal form of love, whereas its opposite, the centripetal motion of love called *eros*, was rejected as demeaning. Contemporary philosophers contend that love of the self is a necessary condition for love of the other. Tillich points out that, although eros begins in the self, it is not merely ego-centric but is the power that leads men to God. If eros is condemned as pseudo-love, then love of God becomes merely obedience. Since one cannot love God without loving others nor love others without loving oneself, love of self and love of the other must be in coincidence.[9]

According to Aristotle, love is love of the good, that which all men desire. Each man desires his *to be*, that which makes him to be rather than not to be. To love another is to increase oneself in being. Aquinas adds to these ideas the important fact that, since all men desire their *to be* and their to be depends upon God, their good and God must be equated. If man loves and thereby gains in being, it is because God is Being itself and the source of love.

Aquinas' theory of love was the paradigm for most of the treatises on love for the next six centuries. Incorporating later Greek (Platonic and Aristotelian) notions of love into a Christian framework, Aquinas presents us with a summation of the theories of love up to his day. For example, the beloved's power to attract the lover was adopted from Plato's notion of participation. Because the beloved participates in God's goodness, the beloved is the good and the final cause of love. Because God is good, each being that God creates, acts as a final cause drawing others to itself.

What is the motivating force of love? Although physical beauty first attracts the lover, it is the beloved's motion toward the good, i.e., his or her way of being, that appeals to the lover. The lover wishes to unite with one who shares his values. This is borne out by Maslow's studies of self-actualizing persons. He says that "in healthy people homogamy is the rule with respect to such character traits as honesty, sincerity, kindliness, and courage."[10]

Aquinas defines love as a circular motion beginning in the beloved who, as the good or final cause, attracts the lover. (In mutual love both the man and woman play the role of lover and of beloved.) The lover, as efficient cause, then joins the beloved in his or her motion toward the good. And finally they unite in the joy of love.

Aquinas mentions three stages of love. In the first stage the beloved attracts the lover. Bringing the lover's "will into tune with his own, he makes it vibrate to his own rhythm, and thus sets up a harmony and a fraternity between these two which are love's first trait."[11] The lover is enticed and longs to join the beloved. Love is not a possession but a convergence of motions. The beloved is coming-to-be in his or her motion toward the good, i.e., he or she is fulfilling values which lead to infinite Good, as in the following diagram:

The Dimension of Love

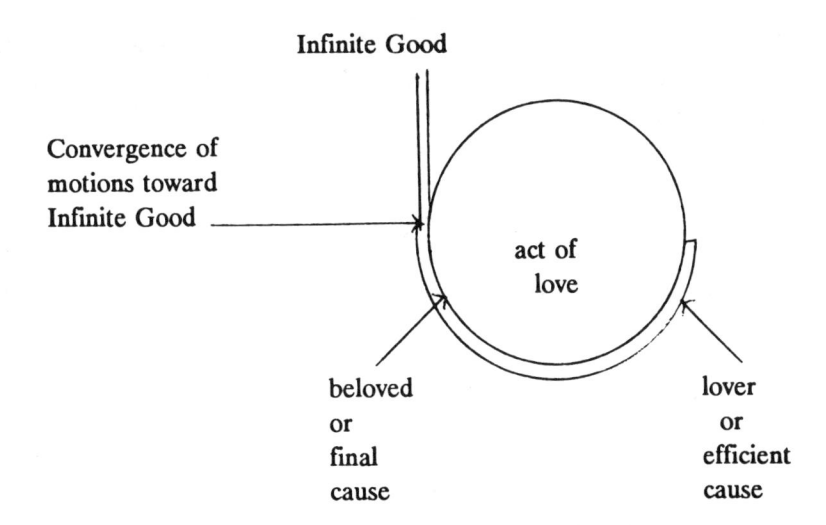

```
                    Infinite Good
                         │
Convergence of           ↓
motions toward          ╱─────╲
Infinite Good  ────→   │ act of │
                       │  love  │
                        ╲─────╱
              beloved              lover
                or                   or
              final               efficient
              cause                 cause
```

In the second stage of love, the lover decides to act upon his desire to join the beloved or to forego it. He consents to his choice or he dissents from it. This is a self-reflective act and is a free choice. If love is not free, according to traditional philosophy, it is not love. It is contradictory to the nature of love for either the beloved or the lover to force the decision to love. The lover is not determined by the beloved nor does he act instinctively but bases his decision upon what he desires in the way of a value system. Even though he is enticed by the beloved, he may dissent to this choice. For example, although the lover may be attracted to the beloved, he may not make this choice because it would prohibit fulfilling his career. If the lover consents to his desire, he will take suitable measures to unite with the beloved.

In the third stage of love, the convergence of the motions of beloved and lover is complete but not completed. Since the end of love is union, the love actively continues. Mouroux says:

> The ultimate condition of love is that the lovers should be linked to a profound fraternity in their very beings...and love is so much the more sovereign, total and intense as the union in question is the more radical.[12]

The converging motions of lover and beloved toward the good result in the positive emotions of longing, desire, and joy. If the good is difficult to obtain, hope is added to longing and courage is added to desire. The emotions that accompany non-love are negative such as hate, anger, sorrow, and so forth. Happiness is the principle of all of the other emotions, according to Aquinas, but it is not in itself that which we desire as is commonly believed. It is the good that we desire and happiness is the concomitant emotion that we experience when we achieve it. If we have our choice between the better or the best, we will choose the best. The less limited the good, the more we desire it. Since it is only God who is infinite good, it is only God who can give us complete happiness.

Emotion is the result of a *motion* toward or away from the good and is therefore produced by the one making the motion. If one desires the beloved as a useful good, i.e., an I-It relation, then the emotion accompanying the motion will be correspondingly short-lived. However, if we love the other for his sake, i.e., an I-Thou relation, the love will grow as there is no reason for it to ever diminish. The I-Thou relation is eternal. The more radical the motion toward the good, the more intense the emotion that accompanies it. Passion is the prerogative of the saint not the sinner.

Since emotion follows upon motion and since we control the motion of love, we indirectly control our emotions. We cannot directly change our emotions, but we have control over them indirectly by the actions we choose. For example, if someone treats us unjustly, although we initially feel anger, instead of taking action against him, we can do something kind for him. Irrespective of how our action is received, we will find that, rather than hatred, we will experience a positive emotion. Buber notes that feelings dwell within man, but man dwells within his love. In love we choose to choose this person, not *in spite of* but *even though* he is unfriendly to us. We leave open the avenues of communication and may even make possible a future friendship. If the person is unable to reciprocate the friendship we have shown him, he is indeed a person in need of our love. Jesus points out that it is within our capacity to love even those who hate us:

> For if you love them which love you, what thank have you?
> ... But love your enemies, and do good, and lend, hoping for nothing again; and your reward will be great.[13]

To be able to reverse a negative emotion into a positive emotion is one of the most rewarding attributes of the human person. In experiencing our deliberate alteration of our emotions, we become aware of our freedom to come-to-be as we choose to be. Rather than being subject to emotions that others arouse in us, we can foster our own feelings. Since we freely choose the motions we make, our emotions, too, are created by us. Emotions don't just happen to us. Whether we are miserable or happy is up to us. Zest for life is self-generated.

Love as a Coincidence of Opposites According to Contemporary Philosophy

Contemporary philosophy emphasizes the coincidence of contraries that gives love its holistic character. Contraries such as active/passive, positive/negative are reconciled by the self so that it is the whole person who loves and is loved, making love an all encompassing experience.

What is the motivating force of love, according to contemporary philosophy? Aquinas believed that "the love which one has for another proceeds from a likeness to the love one has for oneself."[14] But this traditional notion is contested by contemporary surveys indicating that one loves another not as an alter-ego but in his uniqueness as different from the self. For Maslow, it is difference rather than sameness that inspires the love of self-actualizing persons. They

> are not threatened by differences nor by strangeness. Indeed, they are rather intrigued than otherwise.... As for opposites attracting, this is true for my subjects to the extent that I have seen honest admiration for skills and talents which they themselves do not possess. Such superiorities

make a potential partner *more* rather than less attractive to my subjects, whether in man or in woman.[15]

Respect for the same values continues to play an important part in a love relation but different backgrounds and capabilities do not detract but rather add to love.

Contrary to materialism, qualities are not isolated and tabulated, but the person is loved for his own sake in an I-Thou relation. As Kierkegaard notes, to pick and choose among qualities disregards the subjectivity of the loved one, treating him or her as an object. In real love, qualities can diminish or disappear without alteration of the love itself.

> Love's not Time's fool, though rosy lips and cheeks
> Within his bending sickle's compass come;
> Love alters not with his brief hours and weeks
> But bears it out even to the edge of doom.
>
> Shakespeare

One of the vacuities of a materialist age is its lack of respect and appreciation for older persons. Because the society focuses on material goods, the beauty of a loving and kind personality is often disregarded. As artists of all ages have recognized, the face of an elderly person expresses the beauty and wisdom of a life well lived.

True love is not analytical. Its purpose is not to separate but to join. It is experienced through spontaneous subjective intuition which, though it can be mistaken, possesses certitude and is capable of spontaneous action. In the desire to be scientific, the value of understanding based on love is often underestimated. Nevertheless, it is invaluable since it makes possible harmony between persons who otherwise could not arrive at an understanding of each other, such as between intraracial groups. Love is not reserved for crisis situations but the soul of love is in all of the *little* things that one does on a daily basis. An anonymous poem reminds us that love cherishes the little signs of caring, even though we may not show our appreciation at the time.[16]

THINGS YOU DIDN'T DO

Remember the day I borrowed your brand new car and I dented it? I thought you'd kill me,

But you didn't.

And remember the time I dragged you to the beach, and you said it would rain. And it did. I thought you'd say, "I told you so,"

But you didn't.

Do you remember the time I flirted with all those guys to make you jealous, and you were? I thought you'd leave me,

But you didn't.

Do you remember the time I spilled strawberry pie all over your car rug? I thought you'd hit me.

But you didn't.

And remember the time I forgot to tell you the dance was formal and you showed up in jeans? I thought you'd drop me,

But you didn't.

Yes, there were lots of things you didn't do,
But you put up with me, and you loved me, and you protected me.

There were lots of things I wanted to make up to you when you returned from Viet Nam.

But you didn't.

Love is all pervasive, reaching into the very center of our being. Even though we are consciously engaged in our work, love is in the background waiting to express itself when our mind is free. It is the very sustenance by which we live. It is extended to all, from parent to child and child to parent, from teacher to student and student to teacher, from friend to friend and from friend to enemy. Love does not overlook, but looks-over, the faltering of the other, lending a helping hand where needed or showing sympathy or forgiveness. The parents' love for their child sustains him throughout his life and even in the event of their death, it is the memory of them that makes his achievements rewarding. Since love is an increase in being, it is by loving the other and by being loved that we feel the enhancement of our being. Luijpen notes that "The other's love gives me to myself, if this being-myself is understood as a kind of fullness of being."[17] This is particularly true in God's love for us since the complete fulfillment of our being can only be realized through God's gift of himself.

Our gratitude transcends to Being itself as the source of our love. Love is triune, including God as well as well as the lovers. Elizabeth Barrett Browning expresses this beautifully in Sonnet VI.

> What I do
> And what I dream include thee, as the wine
> Must taste of its own grapes.
> And when I sue God for myself,
> He hears that name of thine,
> And sees within my eyes the tears of two.

Love is characterized by its devotion to all persons in God. Love overcomes isolation by breaking away from the one-sidedness of egocentrism. Luijpen notes that love begins as an an appeal to "be with me." It is an invitation to transcend oneself in the unity of love. But love speaks softly; it does not command but merely invites. Those lost in egocentrism are oblivious to its call. If the lover can inwardly respond to the appeal of the beloved, he can overcome his loneliness by accepting the beloved's invitation to share a world.

The Dimension of Love

In mutual love a new world is created which encompasses the worlds of both lover and beloved. Through the other's love my world becomes our world, a world to make our home.

> My world is re-created by the other's love... By means of his affection he wants me to have my world, so that the world shows itself to me in its mildest way and becomes accessible to me without offering resistance. Through the other's love my world becomes my *Heimat*, my country; through it I feel at home in my world, and love it.[18]

Although this new world of love is a real world rather than an idealized world, it is without the limitations of everydayness; "I love thee to the depth and breadth and height my soul can reach," says Elizabeth Barrett Browning. It is expansive through the creativity of love.

Love participates in the self-project of the other. Scheler states:

> the person of another can only be disclosed to me by *my joining in the performance of his acts*, either cognitively, by understanding and vicarious *re-living*, or morally, by *following* in his footsteps.[19]

Love is not disinterested but shares the good fortunes and the misfortunes encountered by the other. Whether parent, teacher, or friend, one participates in the other's projection toward the future by believing in his potential and encouraging him to realize his destiny. Rather than *jumping in* and dominating the other so that he is thrown out of his own position, solicitude is authentic if it *jumps ahead* of the Thou, clearing the way so the Thou will be free to realize his or her possibilities. It then frees the other for himself.[20]

Since it is only in relation that we are truly ourselves, it is only through love that we can overcome non-being and attain our authentic selfhood. The united effort of two lovers creates a more rewarding world than is possible through the effort of two single persons. Love overcomes non-being by maximizing potential. If a person is not productive in other spheres of his life, he will not be successful in love either. By sustaining hope and by encouraging endurance, the partner's support makes a difficult task much easier to accomplish. Nèdoncelle states,

> The will to advance the beloved is demanding: it tolerates neither pettiness nor laziness; it leads us much farther and higher than we had suspected at first; it implies, in effect, an unlimited development of the *I* and *thou*; and in the personal identity it pledges to confer on the lovers, it is the identity and development of all conscious beings that it is logically committed to promote, step by step, to the point where there is a mutual interpenetration of all by God and God by all.[21]

In love each partner is devoted to helping his partner fulfill his destiny. The word *destiny* does not imply something decreed beforehand but that which is elected through the active development of talents and capabilities. Each loves the other, not as imposing his or her particular will upon the partner but accepting the role each has chosen for himself or herself. Each actively wills the world chosen by the partner, helping him to realize his full potential.

Love sometimes calls for a negative response to the other. It refuses to be part of anything that would cause a limitation to the other's self-project. Luijpen notes that "love wants the other's subjectivity, his free self-realization, but this implies that love refuse, precisely because it is love, whatever could impede or destroy the other's possibility of self-realization."[22] It refuses to show itself open to the other's arbitrariness. Both *yea* and *nay* are evidence of love. But one cannot say *no* to the other until one can say *no* to oneself, which requires that one overcome his or her ego-centrism.

Passive acceptance as well as active commitment are integral parts of love. In ancient China, the contraries of yin/yang typified woman as the passive earthly principle and man as the active heavenly principle. But this is to pattern the human person after the physical properties of nature. For contemporary philosophy, in order to fulfill himself or herself, each partner must engage in active and passive roles, divided more or less equally between them. How this division of responsibilities will be made is entirely up to the couple concerned. For example, one marriage worked out very well with the wife employed outside of the home while the husband stayed home to care for the children. This suited her more than housework and it gave him time to exercise his talent as a writer. Unfortunately, society tries to set a stereotyped pattern for the marriage rather than leaving these question to be determined by the marriage partners.

Jung does not see a passive role as optimum for woman. She longs for greater consciousness "which would enable her to name her goal and give it meaning, and thus escape the blind dynamism of nature."[23] He believes it is the role of woman as motivated by Eros "to unite what Logos has sundered." He predicts that, with the recognition that woman should have a more active role, a world free from the ravages of war will become a possibility. "The woman of today," says Jung, "is faced with a tremendous cultural task - perhaps it will be the dawn of a new era."[24] If a woman's strength can only be found by imitating man, however, a change in direction will not likely come about.

Love will be transformed, according to the poet R. M. Rilke, only when human love is seen to be the joining of two unique beings, not stereotyped in their roles of male and female, but loving each other in their humanity. This will be effectuated when each has respect for the other. The word *respect* comes from the word *recipere*, to look into, to search for the most intimate ground of the loved one, to observe his or her uniqueness rather than to pre-judge on the basis of a stereotype.

Discussing the effect of an overly passive role, the psychologist Karen Horney draws attention to what she considers to be a neurotic trend characterized by a strong dependency upon the partner to fulfill the needs of the ego.[25] These *hollow people*, as Rollo May calls them, over-value love as a panacea for fulfilling all of the ego's expectations. Fortunately, this has lessened in this era in that a woman has more opportunity to enhance her ego with her own accomplishments. Horney says that, since the *hollow person* will not work to fulfill his or her own destiny, the partner's success is the only enhancement the ego experiences. This results in an unconscious attempt to exercise covert control over the partner to ensure the fulfillment of the ego's expectations. With dependency ever increasing, an unconscious hostility toward the partner develops. Since the *hollow person* refuses to engage in any self-initiated or sustained activities because of a strong fear of incompetence, a sense of inferiority is the inevitable outcome. There may be even a subtle eroding of the other's stature through innuendoes. This form of pseudo-love does not overcome non-being since it lacks the courage of true love. It will not venture out for the sake of itself or for others and, therefore, is not sufficiently creative to bring love into being.

The unity of love will also miscarry, according to Horney, if the *I* is bent on self-aggrandizement. In this event, there is a tendency toward exploitation of others with an attempt to control them through sheer will power. Or it may take a more innocuous form as a desire to dominate others through covert intellectual superiority, either for personal admiration or for social prestige. With no concern except for one's own advancement, the other is considered at best a stepping stone to one's own achievement. Whereas real love is unitive, self-aggrandizement leads to seclusion and secrecy with a wariness of anything that might intrude into one's privacy. Horney says that instead of the person becoming strong by his efforts, "the tables are actually reversed: it is not that he has will power, but that it has him."[26]

Our ability to practice fidelity to a loved one is prior to and the ground of our ability to integrate the self. Jaspers points out that the "exclusive love of an individual or an unconditional readiness for such love is the sincerity of the spirit of selfhood."

> Exclusiveness in the love of the sexes binds two human
> beings together unconditionally for the whole of their future.
> It is unfathomably rooted in the decision which links the self
> to this fidelity at the moment when it really became aware
> of itself through the other.[27]

Fidelity is possible only by renunciation of polygamous eroticism. But this renunciation is sincere only if it includes the whole of life, according to Jaspers. "The negative determination not to squander oneself is the outcome of an uncompromising readiness for this loyalty on the part of a possible selfhood."[28] Self-realization comes with the ability to focus our being rather than letting it be dispersed into a multitude of wayward goals.

A modicum of jealousy provides protection against an interloper and aids the partner in maintaining his or her fidelity. Since marriage is a commitment to the partner and, in addition, is the matrix from which care of the offspring is provided, no intrusion into its privacy is warranted. The nuclear family should be respected not only for its own sake but as the basis of social institutions. But jealousy can be deleterious if one wishes to keep the partner for one's own as if he or she were a material possession. If one has a commitment to the partner for the partner's sake, then it will be realized that his world will be the richer for his caring for many. Nèdoncelle notes that the partner will not be infinitely lovable unless he infinitely loves the universe of persons and makes himself worthy to be loved by them. "The human love of one person leads to the love of all persons."[29] Whereas romantic love excludes others, true love reaches out to others. The greater the capacity for love, the more the partner will be able to expand his world, not only to care for his immediate family but for an ever widening circle of others in need. We cannot overcome non-being if, instead of loving, we are indifferent to the other. The cruelty of indifference inflicted upon another is, in some instances, much greater for him or her to bear than the death of the loved one.

A certain amount of anger protects our world-model against on onslaught from those who would deny us the freedom to realize our own possibilities. But hatred is a negative emotion which has no useful purpose since its aim is to deny another's right to a world-model of their own. Hatred does not necessarily mean a feeling of aggressiveness against the other. To take pleasure in speaking disparagingly of the other or to ignore him is a more common form of hatred. Hatred usually indicates incapability of dealing in a constructive manner with what we consider to be an unjust situation.

Communication is essential in a love relationship. If one of the partners obstinately hangs on to his or her world-view, thinking it is the only true one, he will be incapable of making needed changes and communication will break down. It takes courage and flexibility, characteristics human beings are often short of, to change the way we have formed our world. It is important to remember that we can adjust to a real world, even though it may have many hardships, but an unreal world sooner or later, like a house built on sand, will come crashing down around us. If we form our world so that it centers around the ego and obstinately hang onto a view that is proven to be wrong, we destroy the possibility of communication. An encounter with those of a different world-model should be looked upon as a challenge. If, by extending our world-model, we can exercise greater love and justice, we should welcome this change.

A too optimistic world-view causes us to believe that human nature is perfect so that we are caught by surprise and angered when we find human failure. On the other hand, by formulating our world too pessimistically, we read into an acceptable situation a negative content which arouses our wrath. We can reconcile ourselves to these situations by realizing the finiteness of man. Trying to understand an evil act is useless, since evil is the absence of being and hence is unintelligible. To give up on a person because of his failings may lead us to give up on ourself. If we believe change is impossible for the other, it may be because we ourselves are unwilling to change. A coincidence of the opposites of optimism and pessimism about human nature gives us a realistic appraisal of human frailty combined with respect for the profound resources of the human person, making it possible for us to "forgive and forget." This, however, requires what Horney calls a "normal" person who is sufficiently flexible to understand and accept the right of others to form their world in a way different from our own. As long as it upholds justice, a unique world model is not only acceptable but enriches human experience.

Horney explains the difference between the *normal* person who can learn to cope with difficult situations and a person with neurotic tendencies who needs help in overcoming his or her problems. The latter is characterized by "a certain rigidity in reaction and a discrepancy between potentialities and accomplishments."[30] There is a tendency to react to all persons in the same way, e.g., through suspicion, spite, and so forth. In addition, although the person may be very intelligent and creative, he is not productive and has considerable fear about his capacity to create. According to Horney, it is anxiety and the defenses built up against it that are the motor which "sets the neurotic process going and keeps it in motion." Rather than heeding the call of conscience and developing our potentiality, there is an attempt to submerge anxiety so that no action to realize possibilities need be taken. It takes courage to let go of the model which originates in the *they* of publicness and develop the unique self that stands on its own merits.

According to Binswanger, it is only when we perceive our weaknesses in relation to our world-model that the prognosis for overcoming them looks promising. "The symptom proves to be the expression of a spreading change of the soul, a change of the total form of existence and the total style of life."[31] He notes that we have a tendency to rationalize a false world-model built upon flights of fancy that gives us a momentary high, only later to thrust us into a bottomless pit. To create for ourselves a world-model that gives us inspiring things to do, demanding intense effort on our part but not exceeding our capacity, will provide the best possibility of living a rewarding life. Jaspers says that "if today we ask in our despair what is still left for us in this world, to every one there comes the answer: 'That which you are, because you can.'" There is open to man the supreme possibility of freedom that he must grasp even in the face of discouragement or accept the alternative of sinking into nullity. It is in communication with others that Jaspers finds the solution to today's meaninglessness. We must see our relation to others as the only possible way of life or be depersonalized. Jaspers does not see this as an easy task for man.

> The demands made of him are such as assume him to have the powers of a titan. He must meet these demands, and must see what he is capable of in the way of self-development; for, if he fails to do so, there will remain for him nothing but a life in which he will have the advantages neither of man or of beast.[32]

Love respects all persons regardless of age, race, or creed. It is a reflection upon the materialism of our culture that the aged, rather than commanding our respect for their wisdom, are perceived to be a burden to society. To place the elderly in homes for the aged deprives grandchildren of the rich and varied experience of their grandparents. Statistics reveal that there is a shorter life span among those who are forced to enter a home for the aged. Children, too, should be treated with respect and given the reason why they are requested to do something. Ordering them to act without explanation teaches the child blind obedience with no more expectations of him than of an animal.

If we increase our ability to love we are also serving the common good of the world. Sorokin, who has made an intensive study of the effects of love on society, concludes that love stops aggression, enmity, and cruelty. Since all of us are human beings, we all are entitled to human rights. Justice is the observation of those rights. In addition, love tempers justice with mercy. Sorokin notes that "a society bound together by coercive bonds is but the worst *prison* society permeated by mutual hate, deprived of any freedom, joyless and drab."[33] Domination over others ignores the possibility of communication that love offers. There is no excuse for ruthless domination of authority. A government can only be effective when it acts on behalf of its people. For example, the so-called People's Republic of China in 1989 showed itself to be, not for its people, but for the leaders who ruthlessly murdered student demonstrators who asked only that their voice be heard on behalf of their country. It is typical of the domination of immaterialist power that it will not listen to any ideas that might in any way contest the validity of its own theory. Yet its own position is tenable, not because it is true, but because it is enforced through fear. With strict prohibition of a free press, the government was able to spread untrue rumors, accusing the students of the violence that it itself was committing. If the government had listened to the voice of the people, it could have added some very badly needed amendments, fostering human rights rather than running counter to them. Instead, students were shot down outright or, without being shown mercy or given a fair trial, were hunted down and sentenced to death. That the government did not consider the students as persons, but merely as obstacles to be removed, is shown by Senior Leader Deng Xiaoping's statement that, to counter the opposition, he would have to spill some blood. The students' answer was: You have tanks; we have blood, pointing out that they were willing to sacrifice their blood, the blood of a human being, for their country, whereas the Politburo, rather than have their *perfect* theory contested, hid behind tanks. Sorokin states: "these machineries, ... persecutions, intolerance, and hypocrisy are the negation and perversion of the power of love...."[34]

This event raises the question: Since rights belong to the human race and not to any select group, is a country interfering in the internal affairs of an errant country to use whatever just methods at its disposal in an attempt to stop the authorities from denying rights to their people? If a man were to beat or murder his wife or children, should this be considered a private affair or should he be held accountable? It appears clear that the common rights of mankind would determine that the man is accountable for his actions. In like manner, since rights belong to humanity rather than to a particular person or persons, it is the concern of all governments and peoples to do whatever just action can be taken to prevent a transgression of human rights wherever it might occur. Members of the Congress of the United States, for example, appealed to China, asking for clemency for the Chinese students who were protesting against the corruption of the Communist government. Since the request was blatantly ignored, the President of the United States placed sanctions upon the Chinese government. Many other countries, as well, vehemently protested this injustice. But heads of state all too soon forget, and protestation on the part of nations will not be entirely effective until each and every person takes it upon himself to observe the rights of others. Unless we learn to love our neighbor as our self, exercising justice and mercy toward all men, we will not be able to bring about a new era of peace. Sorokin notes:

> A society of individuals bound together by a love relationship...is the freest society.... It is the most peaceful and harmonious society; it is also the most creative, most beautiful, and noblest. The love relationship is not only the best, but its minimum is absolutely necessary for long and enjoyable existence of human society....[35]

It is often said that a society is not better than its members. This means that the individual person needs to make every effort possible to fulfill his own potential to help others. We sometimes believe that what we do as a single person will not account for much. But in the experiment on obedience to an authority, it was demonstrated, that if one person desists from obeying an unjust command, over 90% of those present will follow suit as opposed to over 50% who otherwise would have acted unjustly. Heidegger notes that "Dasein is essentially for the sake of others." It is a deficient mode of being when we are only for our own sake and are forgetful of others. Einstein points out that the delusion restricting us to our personal desires and to affection for a few persons nearest to us is a kind of prison from which we must free ourselves by "widening our circle of compassion to embrace all living creatures and the whole of nature in its beauty." Expanding our consciousness to be aware of the needs and interests of others is to grow in love. St. Paul's notion of love is perennial:

> Love is patient; love is kind and envies no one, love is never boastful, nor conceited, nor rude; never selfish, nor quick to take offense. Love keeps no score of wrongs; does not gloat over other men's sins, but delights in the truth. There is nothing love cannot face; there is no limit to its faith, its hope, and its endurance.
>
> I Corinthians 13:46

By choosing the path of love, we approach the dimensionless dimension of eternal life.

Summary

Materialism

> Presupposition: Man acts by instinct (reward and punishment).
>
> Question: If man acts by instinct, what is love?
>
> Conclusion: Love is an I-It relation, i.e., the useful good - lasting only as long as it affords pleasure.

Immaterialism

Presupposition: The intelligible Forms are the true good.

Question: What is human love?

Conclusion: Human love is a stepping stone to love of the Forms (or some "ism").

Traditional Philosophy

Presupposition: Infinite Good is the source of love for finite beings.

Question: What is love for the human person?

Conclusion: The proportionate motions of persons moving toward infinite Being by means of compatible value systems.

Contemporary Philosophy

Presupposition: Lived experience discovers the belonging together of Dasein and Being.

Question: How does love encourage the belonging together of Dasein and Being?

Conclusion: Love is working together to help all persons realize their destiny in God.

1. Martin Buber, *I and Thou*, trans. R. G. Smith (New York: Scribner Son's, 1958), p. 34

2. Rollo May, *Love and Will* (New York: W. W. Norton, 1967), p. 97

3. Ibid.

4. Sophocles, "Antigone," *The Complete Greek Tragedies*, ed. D. Gren and R. Lattimore (Chicago: University of Chicago Press, 1957), II, 780-800

5. Jean Guitton, *Human Love*, (Chicago: Franciscan Herald Press, 1966), p.21

6. Ibid., p. 173

7. Thomas Gould, *Platonic Love* (New York: Free Press of Glencoe, 1963), p. 53

8. Carl G. Jung, *Psyche and Symbol*, ed. V.S. de Laszlo (Garden City, New York: Doubleday, 1958), pp. 12-16

9. Paul Tillich, *Love, Power, and Justice* (Oxford: Oxford University press, 1960), p. 28

10. Abraham Maslow, "Love in Healthy People," *The Practice of Love*, ed. A. Montague (Englewood Cliffs, New Jersey: Prentice Hall, 1975), p. 111

11. Jean Mouroux, *The Meaning of Man*, trans. A. H. G. Downes (Garden City, New York: Doubleday, 1961), p. 187

12. Ibid., p. 184

13. Luke: 27-35

14. Aquinas, III *Sentences* 28, 16c

15. Maslow, "Love in Healthy People," in Montague, *Practice* ..., p.111

16. Leo Buscaglia, *Living, Loving & Learning*, ed. Steven Short (New York: Holt, Rinehart and Winston, 1982), pp. 75-76

17. William A. Luijpen, *Existential Phenomenology* (Pittsburgh: Duquesne University Press, 1965), p. 229

18. Ibid., p. 30

19. Max Scheler, *The Nature of Sympathy*, trans. P. Heath (London: Routledge & Kegan Paul, 1970), p. 167

20. Heidegger, *Being and Time*, p. 158

21. Maurice Nèdoncelle, *Love and the Person*, trans. R. Adelaide (New York: Sheed & Ward, 1966), p. 30

22. Luijpen, *Existential Phenomenology*, p. 219

23. Jung, *Civilization in Transition*, p. 312

24. Ibid., p. 133

25. Karen Horney, "The Neurotic Need for Affection," *The Neurotic Personality of Our Time* (New York: W. W. Norton, 1964), pp. 102-161

26. Ibid., "The Quest for Power, Prestige and Possession," *The Neurotic Personality...*, pp. 162-206

27. Karl Jaspers, *Man in the Modern Age*, trans. E. Paul and C. Paul (London: Routledge & Kegan Paul, 1966), p. 185

28. Ibid.

29. Nèdoncelle, *Love and the Person*, p. 60

30. Horney, *Neurotic Personality*, p. 22

31. Ludwig Binswanger, *Existence*, ed. R. May, E. Angel and H. F. Ellenberger (New York: Basic Books, 1958), p. 213

32. Jaspers, *Man in the Modern Age*, pp. 176-177

33. Pitirim Sorokin, *The Ways and Power of Love* (Chicago: Henry Regnery, 1965), p. 76

34. Ibid., p. 72

35. Ibid., p. 76

Chapter VII

THE DIMENSIONLESS DIMENSION

Throughout the history of mankind, man has longed to transcend himself - to enter the dimensionless dimension. The quest for a haven or heaven beyond the dimension of time and space in which our inquiring mind can find satisfaction and our desire for fulfillment be realized is present in the most primitive of peoples. For materialism, death is the cessation of life. Any belief in a dimension beyond the physical is held in contempt because it is not visible to the senses. But because it belongs to the very heart of what it means to be a human being, the question of eternal life cannot be glossed over as if it were an idle dream. Nor can the question of God be overlooked for, in the words of the Islamic Hallaz, God is "more intimate to the soul than the soul is to itself." The measured has little or no meaning without consideration of the immeasurable.

The Meaning of Death

It is the possibility of death that brings to light the question of the meaning of our being and makes us aware of a dimensionless dimension. Being itself, as the immeasurable, measures us by summoning us to death.[1] Heidegger, probably more than any other philosopher, has made death one of the central issues of his philosophy. As a *pro-ject* toward the future, we are related to death in our very being. It is because death is the contradictory of possibility in the time and space dimension that we are made aware of an end point from which the present takes shape. As the shrine of non-being, death is the highest redoubt (the gathering concealment) of the mystery of Being.[2] It conceals Being, in the sense that it brings to finality the time dimension, and yet reveals Being by invoking in us the question, What does it mean to be? Death reveals to us that our being is not exhausted by everydayness but transcends time and space in the mystery of Being.

Heidegger notes that contemporary man lost in publicness flees death. Inauthentic Dasein, lost in the *they* of everydayness, speaks of death in a fugitive manner as if it had nothing to do with him until the event of death.

We even attempt to talk the dying person into believing that he will escape death. Rather than give meaning to death, we try to maintain constant tranquilization about it. On the other hand, authentic Dasein realizes that an anticipatory understanding of death makes possible the realization of its present individuality. Knowing that one must face death alone makes us aware that life, too, exacts personal responsibility.

> Death is *Dasein's* ownmost possibility. Being towards this possibility discloses to Dasein its ownmost potentiality-for-Being, in which its very Being is the issue.[3]

Because we face death alone, we realize our uniqueness, that we are accountable not to others but to ourselves, a realization that should be present to us not just in death but throughout our lifetime.

Death is a constant reminder of the finiteness of Dasein - that we can transcend our finiteness only by relating to Being itself. If we have our only identity in everydayness, in the *they* of idleness and egocentrism, death will appear to us as the non-being we have lived. But if we live our life with enthusiasm, open to the disclosure of itself that Being offers to us, we will face death with the anticipation with which we have lived our earthly life. Kierkegaard notes that unfortunately our age is lacking in passion and "too tenacious of life to die, for dying is one of the most remarkable leaps... a blessed leap into eternity."[4] Death is not the cessation of life but the beginning of a new dimension.

The Dimension of Eternal Life

In this contemporary age statistics show that approximately 97% of persons believe in an afterlife. Belief is partially based upon the experiences of dying persons. Deathbed visions are common in both eastern and western countries, as indicators of survival after death. Data on such experiences reveal the following facts.[5] Unlike the destruction hypothesis which contends that life experiences determine death experiences, all races and creeds have reported like experiences. Research reveals that sex, age, and education have little influence on the death bed experience and, whereas religion appears to facilitate afterlife experiences, many "who were only slightly involved in religion and did not express a belief in afterlife, still had otherworldly emotions." There was "no relation whatsoever between medication and experiential characteristics suggestive of an afterlife." Mood elevation near the time of death often accompanied visions of oncoming post-mortem existence. Many times a loved one came to carry away the dying person and "not a single apparition involving a phantasm of a living person was described as coming with a take-away purpose." The dying experience a heightened consciousness of those they leave behind in this dimension. Such factual reports, however, neither prove nor disprove immortality.

Immortality is a belief that has persisted throughout the history of mankind. Primitive peoples believed in a separate soul which leaves the body at death. The ancient Egyptians believed that the soul is a manikin, i.e., a little man which resembles its owner in every detail.[6] The natives of Yap in the South Pacific conceive of the soul as an invisible body dwelling within the visible body, resembling it in form exactly.[7] The people believe that during sickness, dreams, madness, and even childbirth, if precautions are not taken to close up the orifices through which it could escape, there is danger that the soul will fly away and death ensue.

> Hence in the Celebes they sometimes fasten fishhooks to a sick man's nose, navel, and feet, so that if his soul should try to escape it may be hooked and held fast.[8]

Though the notion of the *invisibility* of the soul was more akin to material breath, it represents an attempt to conceive of an eternal soul and demonstrates man's desire to transcend space and time. Traditional philosophers contend that such a desire could not be originated by man unless immortality is possible. In other words, although immortality rests upon desire, desire rests upon real possibility.

The primitive notion of immortality was communal and consisted of a prolongation of the present time and space dimension - the spirits of dead ancestors live on. With Plato, however, the soul was conceived as immortal and hence indestructible. It not only lives prior to its entrance into the body but at death returns to the heaven of perfect forms. In the Phaedo, Socrates says:

> Then since what is immortal is also indestructible, if the soul is really immortal, surely it must be imperishable too. Quite inevitably. So it appears that when death comes to a man, the mortal part of him dies, but the immortal part returns at the approach of death and escapes unharmed and indestructible.[9]

Plato's notion of immortality rests on his theory of reminiscence. Aristotle did not agree with Plato's notion of reminiscence, pointing out that the intellect is a clean slate at birth upon which nothing is written. We know material objects immaterially by means of abstraction. Aristotle still held to man's immortality, however. But because he believed that the soul is the form of the body, there could be no personal immortality. Since it is its relation to the body that individuates the soul, with the death of the body the soul would also lose its individuation.

According to Aquinas, the soul has personal immortality. It is the very *esse* or to be of the human being. It comes-to-be through God's creative power rather than from preexisting matter and although the human person is *individuated* by matter, he is an *individual*, not because of the time and space he occupies, but because his unique spiritual soul was and continues to be created by infinite Being.

Thomas Aquinas accounts for the immortality of the human soul by means of the immaterial nature of its powers. The soul cannot be less than its powers. And since, with our intellectual powers, we perceive things immaterially such as philosophy, justice and so forth, the soul also must be immaterial. Material things are corruptible but the soul, being immaterial, is not subject to the ravages of time and space. He states:

> Likewise, that which properly perfects the soul of man is something incorruptible; for the proper operation of man, as man, is understanding, since it is in this that he differs from brutes, plants, and inanimate things. Now, it properly

> pertains to this act (of the human person) to apprehend objects universal and incorruptible as such. But perfections must be proportionate to things perfectible. Therefore, the human soul is incorruptible.[10]

However since God created the soul, He could destroy it.

After the death of the body will we exist as the persons we are in this time and space dimension? Obviously not, since in a dimensionless dimension we have no need for sense powers. Our way of being will not be limited by the material dimension. According to Berdyaev, eternity is not a prolongation of this life but a dimensionless dimension which exists even now. It is not a heaven existing in limitless space and in endless time.

> The Kingdom of God cannot be thought of as existing in time; it is the end of time, the end of the world, a new heaven and a new earth. But if the Kingdom of God is out of time and in eternity, it cannot be referred entirely to the end of the world, for that end is in time. The Kingdom of God comes not only at the end of time but at every moment. A moment may lead us from time into eternity.[11]

Perhaps this is close to what Jesus means when he says that the kingdom of heaven is "at hand."

Because we are finite we cannot by ourselves enter the dimensionless dimension. It is not natural man that can overcome death, but, according to Christianity, it is those who accept Jesus that are give eternal life. To accept Jesus means to recognize that he paid the penalty to erase our sins. But Jesus will forgive us only if we forgive those who sin against us. "But if ye do not forgive, neither will your father which is in heaven forgive your trespasses." Mark 11,26. For Berdyave the moral imperative is: if you wish to gain courage to face death you should "act so that eternal life might be revealed to you and that the energy of eternal life radiates from you to all creatures."[12] In order for this to take place it is necessary to believe in God.

The Relation of the Human Being to Being Itself

The notion of immortality is explicable only by consideration of the relation of the human being to Being itself. This most basic truth is discovered through our love of God. But what if we do not believe in God? James proposes a way of solving this problem. As beings who are concerned with our being, we have the option to believe in God or not to believe in him. There is no middle ground in this logical disjunction. James points out that the option to believe has three qualities about it that make it worth considering.[13]

1. Since it falls within our horizon of meaning, it is a live option rather than a dead one.

2. Since we either must accept God or refuse him, it is a forced choice rather than an avoidable one.

3. Since it determines the meaning that Being has for us, it is a momentous decision rather than a trivial one.

That this is the most important decision that can be made by the human person is evident from the fact that nothing so alters our own way of being as our relation to Being itself. If we accept infinite Being as the source of all that is, we will live in a real world and truth will be our ally. There are two possible alternatives to belief in God: One can make his ego the apex of his value system, clinging to material possessions or he can give away his responsibility and his freedom to an "ism" as a substitute for God. Since neither looks promising, why would a person choose one or the other?

James looks to personality types to discover why some of us can choose easily and others encounter the question of God's existence as if it were a stumbling block. Attempting to ignore it altogether, the materialist believes that he or she must at all costs avoid error. Such a person hesitates to accept any truth at all for fear of being duped.[14] Placing great emphasis upon factual information, the materialist either rejects God outright or, like

Freud, equates God with an overblown father image. Such skepticism relies upon science as if it were certain knowledge, which it is not, since science devises hypotheses to explain its data. Many materialists fall back upon evolution as a substitute for belief in God. However, evolution cannot be explained without reference to God. Since neither man nor ape created himself, the sufficient reason for their being must be sought in Being itself, the uncaused Cause, who made all others to be. Nor could they evolve from a lower form unless they received an increment in being, which must again be explained by an uncaused Cause. Nor could evolution be attributed merely to chance; for either chance exists in which case it is caused by an uncaused Cause or it does not exist in which case it cannot cause anything. Since the materialist will not rely on his intellectual power because it might be in error, he cannot confront questions concerning the cause of our being. But, as James points out, the risk of being in error is a very small matter compared to the blessings of real knowledge. He suggests we should be ready to be duped many times in our investigations rather than postpone indefinitely the chance of guessing true.

James contends it is our belief in God which makes possible the existence of this truth for us. "Desire for a certain kind of truth here brings about that special truth's existence."[15] For example, if you refused to communicate your love to someone because you were afraid they may not love you, you would lose the loved one even though it were true that he or she does love you. By the same token, if we refuse to communicate our love to God, because we are afraid that he does not exist, we will lose him since we did not let him be for us. Unlike human love, there need not be any fear of not receiving God's love. Since it is with the love God gives us that we are able to love him, we cannot fail to have our love returned.

To discover the real God is a quest that each person must undertake for himself. It is impossible to communicate to another the reality of God. Sometimes, a limited notion of God is handed down from one generation to another and we are alienated from the real person that is God. It has been such a reification of God that has *covered over* the real God and made western man in the last century declare that *God is dead*.

Whether or not we are to equate Being itself with God is answered in the affirmative by those philosophers who seek to explain the origin of man's being. As a reconciliation of the opposites of skepticism and dogmatism, traditional philosophy takes an open attitude toward truth, accepting on faith that which transcends understanding. According to Aquinas, since we did not bring ourselves into existence, we must look to an uncaused Cause to account for our existence. To explain the existence of finite beings we must finally recognize an infinite Being who, itself uncaused, causes all other beings to be. Since our being is contingent, it must be held into existence by a Being who necessarily is, a Being who is pure *esse*, without limitation himself but who can create finite beings. Otherwise there would be an infinite regress and we would never arrive at the source from which beings are created or increase in being. This view is not exclusively western. Huang Po also speaks of the "the self-existent and uncreated Absolute."

Traditional philosophy accepts the above evidence for the existence of God, not as a priori knowledge as in immaterialism, but from what can be learned from our observation of the world in its causality and its complexity. The intelligence we see in the intricate design of natural things, for example, points to an omniscient creator. Salvador Dali, on hearing of the discovery of DNA by Watson and Crick, said, "This is for me the real proof for the existence of God."

It is often questioned, If God is and is perfect, why are there natural catastrophies? Human beings are part and parcel of nature. No earthling could live on a planet with different conditions. For example, without the catastrophic changes that have occurred there would not have been sea plants to provide an ozone layer to protect us from the sun's rays, nor land plants to provide oxygen for us to breathe. Nor can we eliminate extremes since what now is called average would then become extreme. To eliminate extremes it would be necessary to make everything the same and hence static. We might just as well ask why we must have a physical body of this particular kind as to ask why nature is the way it is. God provides us with whatever is necessary for our physical existence. If we take care of nature, harness its energy, and learn to adapt to it, we will feel that this is our world and be grateful for it. Wittgenstein notes that it is not any particular thing that proves the existence of God but that the universe is at all.[16]

It is only by examining the capabilities and the limitations of our mind that philosophy can evaluate the possible extent of our knowledge about

God. We can affirm *that* God is since he is Being itself. However, since we understand the essence of something according to its limitation of being, we cannot say *what* God is or, analogically, it could be said, his essence is his existence which means he is perfection itself without limitation. Whereas traditional philosophy has offered many intellectual proofs for the existence of God, contemporary philosophy continues to search for a a more intimate approach. Since the question of God is also a matter of the heart, it cannot be answered by factual data as in materialism nor by universals as in immaterialism. The reconciliation of the contradictories of being/non-being requires a more personal notion of God than that which is offered by speculative knowledge of God. Philosophers such as Pascal, Kierkegaard, and Jaspers, for example, prefer the *way of the heart*. Speculative knowledge gives us belief *about* God but not belief *in* God.

A Frameless Framework

If every age has believed in God, why then has atheism or agnosticism affected our time? Heidegger refused to consider the question of God at all because he believed that our age "is already so impoverished that it can no longer recognize the absence of God as an absence." Until we have originated a framework from which the question of God can be raised, we cannot find an answer to this question. In losing sight of the immeasureable, the deepest meaning of our being is forfeited. Is it not time for us to take thought in this most *thought-provoking* of times and awaken to our dimensionless dimension?

One of the most important contributions oriental philosophy has made is its absolute refusal to reify the Ultimate or in any manner to limit it. Zen Buddhism points to *That* which is beyond Being, the *ungrund* or ground of all that is. Perhaps by looking into the culture of the Far East we can discover a *frameless* framework which will lend itself to the possibility of our becoming more aware of the Transcendent.

Zen notes that not even with our intellectual power can we point to *That* which is above or underlying all contradictories. To arrive at such a conception, it is necessary to transcend the being/non-being dichotomy of the intellectual power. Maréchal points out, since it is the nature of the intellectual power to adhere to one side of a proposition but not to both, (either Yes, it is or No, it is not) our act of thinking is stopped dead by logical contradiction. In order to know God it is necessary to rise above the natural operation of the intellectual power to realize a coincidence of contradictories. On experiencing Being Itself the Sufi mystic says, "I am what is not. I am, O you who know, the soul in the All." The Sufi's seemingly contradictory saying indicates a meaning beyond that which our intellectual power knows in its natural operation.

It is not possible for our intellectual power itself to break out of the being/non-being dichotomy. In attempting to do so, the circularity of intellectual operation is made evident. If we assert God *is* being and non-being, we are in fact saying God *is not* being and non-being which is a repetition which is contradictory. The reasoning process is itself circular and does not lead to the ground from which it originates. "The denying of reality is the asserting of it and the asserting of emptiness is the denial of it."[17] Lu K'uan Yu recommends: "Cut off the *is* and *is not* and cut off the *neither is* and *neither is not*. But even this cannot be done by the power of intellect. Yet, oriental philosophers say, *That* in "some marvelous way" is and is not. "It is an existence which is no-existence, a non-existence which is nevertheless existence. So this true Void does in some marvelous way *exist*."[18]

The inexpressible is beyond or underlying being as known by intellectual power: yet it *is* in *some marvelous way* the True Reality. It cannot, therefore, be spoken. It includes speech but is at once beyond speech.

Chan-Yen King:	"You discourse ordinarily on the subject of Wu-nien (no-thought or no-consciousness), and make people discipline themselves in it. I wonder if there is a reality corresponding to the notion of Wu-nien or not?"
Shen-Hui:	"I would not say Wu-nien is a reality, nor that it is not."
Chang-yen King:	"Why?"
Shen-Hui:	"Because if I say it is a reality, it is not in the sense in which people generally speak of reality: if I say that it is a non-reality, it is not in the sense which

	people generally speak of non-reality. Hence Wu-nien is neither real nor unreal."
Chang-yen King:	"What would you call it then?"
Shen-hui:	"I would not call it anything."[19]

It is clear that *That* cannot be named or known through words.

Heidegger points out that we could never know the totality of beings. Rather it is Being-in-totality that we know by setting being off against its opposite, non-being. Non-being, by itself, cannot be understood since there is no-thing to be grasped. Rather, we experience nothingness through the mood of dread. When dread seizes us, we are faced with nothing. We do not flee any particular thing but Being-in-totality flees from us. Everything becomes indifferent. We vanish with the receding Being, experiencing total emptiness. At this moment we are totally free to choose our life, to relate to infinite Being in a more comprehensive way or to return to our egotistical ends. To pursue the former we must take a more than intellectual approach to God.

Maréchal notes that the human mind in ever in quest of its union with Being itself.

> The human mind is a *faculty in quest of its intuition*--that is to say, of assimilation with Being, Being pure and simple, sovereignly *one*, without restriction....The affirmation of reality, then, is nothing else than the expression of the fundamental tendency of the mind to unification in and with the Absolute.[20]

Jaspers believes we can know God only by exercising our freedom. The one who attains true awareness of his freedom gains certainty of God, says Jaspers.[21] We can only be free through our capacity for self-determination, i.e., to be the cause of our own actions. As a materialist, I do not admit causality and therefore cannot admit my own freedom. But if I do admit causality, I not only admit my own freedom but also must admit God as uncaused Cause of my freedom. Since it is God who gives us power to act as a cause, it is He who gives us our freedom. According to Jaspers, because *I can*, I know that I am not through myself but am given my freedom from God. God exists for me, insofar as I become authentically myself and I become authentically myself only by acting in freedom. My freedom is gained by my evaluating all in the light of the supreme value, i.e., Good Itself.

The greatest gift of freedom God gives us is the freedom to choose him as our highest good or to choose ourselves. We might question, Why does God give us this choice? Why does he not reveal himself so that, as the good without measure, we could not help but love him? We need but consider, if the choice were ours, would we prefer our children to love us because we force them to or because they freely choose to do so? Freedom to choose God or not to choose him is ensured by the fact that God reveals himself only to those who choose him.

Since we usually operate with the data of our senses as well as our intellect and will, we are seldom if ever aware of our powers when separated from the body and only have glimpses of the eternal life of the spirit. Maréchal notes that the mystical experience is always different from the familiar exercise of either sense perception or reasoning. "The solution of the riddle of life in space and time lies outside space and time." It is clear that the intellect cannot understand that which is beyond differentiation. When the mind is in a state of *wu-nien* or no-thought, it is open to a way that is inexpressible. Since it is ineffable, an account of the mystical experience is very difficult to express in words. Wittgenstein says:

> There is indeed the inexpressible. This shows itself; it is the mystical. What can be shown cannot be said.... What we cannot speak about we must pass over in silence.[22]

The human person, in attempting to transcend himself, demonstrates his present state of incompleteness. Some persons discover this completeness in the state of ecstasy.

Steps to Enlightenment

There are a number of steps various philosophies and religions suggest that can be taken to facilitate man's unity with infinite Being. They are amazingly similar, though from completely different civilizations. Whereas the practices of various religions are to a large extent determined by the varying environments from which they spring, man's nature exceeds environmental influences, and the way to the dimensionless dimension is the same for all men. There is a fourfold path to enlightenment: the practice of commandments; the attainment of emptiness (sunyata); the experience of enlightenment (satori); and finally reentry into the world.

All oriental philosophies as well as the religions of the West prepare the self for enlightenment by teaching their disciples to first strengthen their ego by right practices in order to live in the world in harmony with others. The commandments of Buddhism, for example, are very similar to those of Christianity.[23]

After this period in which the ego is strengthened, it withdraws from worldly attachments in order that the self may predominate. "One should strive to be flexible hollow. Only then can one reach the state of wonder," advises Master Po Shan.[24] This state is called *Sunyata* which literally means emptiness or void. Emptiness is not the equivalent of non-being as is usually believed in the West. Zen has non-being, too, as contradictory to being, but *Sunyata* is beyond being and non-being and must be experienced in an entirely different way. This is a *letting go* of the usual way of knowing in order that the mind experience a *seeing that is no-seeing*. This should not be mistaken for a vacuity of consciousness, which Rinzai Zen criticizes as an impossibility and to be unwise even if it were possible. That Zen opposes shutting out thought is made clear by Hui-neng, the father of Ch'an (Zen) Buddhism.

> Learned friends, there are also those who teach people to sit for the purpose of watching over the mind and of contemplating stillness, without motion and without any uprise in the mind, and who claim that this is real achievement. The deluded man who knows nothing about

this, sticks to it and so becomes insane. There are cases like this. Such a teaching is a great mistake.[25]

Akin to the idea that the mind would be inundated with imaginary figures, is Jesus' saying that a house swept clean will be inhabited by seven devils in place of the one. It is the illusion created around phenomena that needs to become as nothing. This illusion is the *firm ground* upon which one's feet stand when, to the Zen initiate, a mountain is a mountain. This is also similar to the inauthenticity Heidegger warns against. When the mind becomes as void, then a mountain is no longer a mountain. (In the final stage of enlightenment, a mountain again becomes a mountain, not with the *firmness* of factuality, but with the *certitude* of eternality.)

Rinzai Zen meditates in life rather than abstracting from it. Meditation consists in absolving *clinging* to thoughts, allowing only the *rise and fall of consecutive thoughts* without grasping at them as a substitute for reality. "Let your communication be Yea, yea; Nay, nay; for whatsoever is more than these cometh of evil," is of similar directive.[26]

It is the ego that stirs and stops thought in the interest of its own ends; so it is the ego that must become as void. The purpose of our powers is to effectuate the creative processes that originate from the Self-Nature. If the ego serves its own interests it is not at the disposal of the True Self. A claim on the part of the old man prevents the birth of the new (Self-Nature). Just as Jesus taught that one must give up his life in order to gain it, so Zen teaches that one must give up the his old self (or ego) in order to realize his Self-Nature.

> What Huang Po calls the total abandonment of Hsin - mind, thought, perceptions, concepts and the rest - implies the utter surrender of self (ego) insisted on by Sufi and Christian mystics.[27]

Zen points out that it is the excessive demands of the ego that need to become as nothing. Whether we respond to the real world or cling to a world of our own making determines whether or not it will bind us. Thus

Tilpa, teaching his disciple Naropa on the Mahamudra, warns that it is not the world that binds him but his own clinging:

> It is not the manifestations that have bound you in *Saṁsāra*.
> It is the clinging that has tied you down. Oh, it is the clinging that made you - Naropa.[28]

Contrary to western speculation, Zen does not advocate the cessation of all desire. Not willing is an impossibility since to will to not will is also to will. But it is excessive willing and captivated thought that binds one to *Saṁsāra*.

It is the thought of the non-ego which thwarts the ego. For example, we focus our attention upon injustices suffered at the hands of another. We become *fasten*ated by these injustices, engaging in excessive analysis of the motives behind them. But this is futile, because, as an absence of being, i.e., non-being, evil is unintelligible. As long as there is free choice, there will be those who choose the way of injustice. We may engage in vilification of those who are unjust, planning retribution or revenge, but that is to act unjustly to overcome injustice. It is useless to cling to a world which is contradictory. We need to abhor injustice but rise above any personal onslaught. To retain freedom and yet have complete justice is only possible in an unreal world.

Zen, in addition, warns against the contemplation of self-perfection. The repentant conscience clings to such concepts as purity, humility, and others. Hui-neng warns against such a practice:

> When you cherish the notion of purity and cling to it you turn purity into falsehood.... Purity has neither form nor shape and when you claim an achievement by establishing a form to be known as purity, you obstruct your own self-nature, you are purity-bound.[29]

It is only by seeing into the falsity of all claims that one practices humility. The uselessness of seeking perfection is likewise pointed out by the question "Which one of you by taking thought can add one cubit unto his stature?" Only God is perfect. The misquoted phrase, "Be ye therefore perfect..." is more correctly translated: Be ye therefore complete, even as your Father which is in heaven is complete. To be complete is to realize our own potentialities rather than fulfilling an impossible standard of perfection. The willful claims of a wayward ego or the upright claims of a prudent conscience must equally be abandoned.

Let the mind alight nowhere. This is the ideal of all Zen training, achieved when at last attachment to thought is ended, and ideas may be used as tools without becoming so many fetters.[30] This idea approximates Heidegger's call of conscience. On the other hand, traditional philosophy demands that we keep a close surveillance upon our actions to see that they measure up to a standard. The intellect is taken up with justifying every action. There is constant self-recrimination or self-enhancement as one falls short of or attains the standard set for oneself. This is the initial step that one must take to strengthen character, but it is important to go beyond this goal to adhere to Jesus' saying, "Judge not, that ye be not judged." Likewise Zen warns, "Deluded men practice blessed virtues, not the truth which they say these virtues are."

By ceasing to cling, the True Man or Self-Nature becomes manifest. But the ego is afraid of the consequences of giving itself over to another power greater than itself, thereby losing its identity, even though this identity be false. The conceptual world-view it has built up places its feet upon *firm* ground. However, Zen, like Christianity, asks that every last farthing be forfeited. It is by our plunging into the darkness of the unknown, that Being manifests itself to us. The state in which one becomes egoless is spoken of by Christian mystics such as St. John of the Cross as the *dark night of the soul*. This is illustrated by Zen Master Hakuin's painting of a monkey hanging precariously from a bough (the monkey is man and the moon symbolizes *That*) to which is added the following verse:

> The monkey is reaching for the moon in the water,
> Until death overtakes him he'll never give up.
> If he'd let go the branch and disappear into the deep pool,
> The whole world would shine with dazzling pureness.[31]

When the ego is stilled and the soul is empty of temporal concerns, it is ready for its unification with the Transcendent. The Muslim mystic

Hallaz says, "There is a selfness of thine which dwells in my nothingness." Since the soul is raised above its natural operation, it is a gratuitous influx of being which brings it to ecstasy.

The Dimensionless Dimension

It is only in this contemporary age that belief in a Transcendent Being has become an issue. In every part of the world historical man has aspired to unite with the transcendent. The description of such an experience is astoundingly similar in all great philosophies and religions whether Infinite Being is referred to as Life Force, That, Buddha Nature, Self Nature, Allah, Being Itself or God. The Chinese philosopher Lao Tzu said, "He who acts in accord with the Tao becomes one with the Tao;" the Indian Buddha said "The dew-drop slips into the shining sea;" the Upanishad reads, "Time ripens and dissolves all beings in the Great Self." Whereas the above are pantheistic in the sense that the self is lost in the Godhead, the preservation of the self in immortality is made evident in the words of Jesus, "...I am in my Father, and ye in me and I in you."[32] Bragdon illustrates this:

> This is the real miracle of the Incarnation, that not only can the drop flow into and become one with the ocean, but that *the ocean can flow into and become one with the drop*; the personality, in losing itself in the life-force, cannot itself be lost.[33]

With the eclipse of the ego, "heaven spins and the earth somersaults," an entirely different realm appears.[34] This realm is a dimensionless dimension with no space or time the mind is completely withdrawn from the body. The soul is united with *That*, which is compared to a lamp whose light is *Prajna*. The Western expressions used to point to the experience of *enlightenment* are similar to those used by eastern mystics. The Holy Bible of Christianity refers to God as light, "...God is light, and in Him is no darkness at all." John 1,5 *That* possesses spiritual brilliance; "it shines forever and on all with the brilliance of its own perfection."[35] Brilliance or light is the terminology most encountered. "One evening during meditation I clearly saw the great Illuminating Whole - pellucid, transparent, void, and clear like a limpid ocean - nothing at all existed!"[36] (*Void* does not mean non-being but that which transcends non-being.)[37] The mystical experience is an immediate and intimate confrontation with the Transcendent. The mystic Van Ruysbroeck calls this an "immediate presence," an overpowering and absolutely new "brightness." It is a penetrating illumination, a blinding light which floods the soul to such an extent that it becomes that light.

> Behold how this secret clarity in which man contemplates all that he has desired, in the manner of the emptiness of the spirit, this clarity is so great that the loving contemplative sees and feels in his depths where he rests, nothing except an incomprehensible light. And according to the manner of this single nakedness which embraces all things, he finds himself and feels himself to be that very light by which he sees, and nothing else.[38]

James considers this consciousness of illumination to be the essential mark of true *mystical states*.

There is no way of knowing whether or not or at what time such an experience will occur. *Prajna*, like the Holy Ghost of Christianity, bloweth where it listeth. All mystics would agree that their unity with the Godhead is a *fait accompli* beyond their initiative. Although very few persons ever experience ecstasy and those who do so generally have only one experience of this kind, it does indicate for all others that the human person can enter the dimensionless dimension and discover his unity with God. Whatever the manner of uniting with infinite Being, it is clear from the history of mankind, that it belongs to the human person to transcend himself. The absolute certitude attending the mystical experience gives us unalterable conviction of the being of God.

According to Maréchal and James, there is one differentiating factor between a real and a pseudo-mystical experience: the former inspires the mystic to render humble service to God. A Bodhisattva, for example, is one who has experienced Satori but returns to earth to help the unenlightened to experience oneness with *That*. For Zen, this is a return to one's original face. "We cannot *become* what we have always been; we can only become intuitively aware of our original state, previously hidden from us by the clouds of maya."[39] For Christianity, it is to return to a state of innocence - in order to enter the kingdom of heaven, one must become like a little child.

Zen does not consider itself to be mysticism because the mystical experience is not its ultimate goal. Zen prefers to see *That* operating in everyday life without even a hair's breadth between *Prajñā* and *saṁsāra* (everyday life). This does not mean that the two become indistinguishable. Hui-neng insists that *Prajñā* and *saṁsāra* retain their identity. The Christian notion that one should live in the world but not of the world is similar. The self is united with Being and acts by inspiration of the eternal. This is akin to Meister Eckhart's hinge in which the self remains stationary in the light of the eternal while the ego or handle of the door swings to and fro taking care of worldly affairs. If Satori is the moon in the heavens, then Zen considers full awakening to come about only with the descent of the moon (when a mountain is again a mountain). The Zen master comes back to sit among the coal and ashes. Enlightenment must be the pearl "found in the marketplace" not just in another realm. "Ah, it is a jewel beyond all price!" says Huang Po;[40] yet it is present in the most common experience.

A person is not completely enlightened until the experience of *Satori* has been laid aside in order that its light "permeates the four corners." Since all beings are then seen with the same inner eye, the stage of no-mindedness is attained in which one cares for the other in the same no-thought manner that one cares for oneself, without discrimination of any kind. He takes up his work of aiding others to awaken to *That*. Hakuin Ekaku advises:[41]

> Who has the jointed bridge of Mama
>   in his heart,
>   Him would I have throw it
>   across the world of men.

This dimensionless dimension is a coincidence of opposites. "In the midst of contraries clear understanding wins the day." Nothing is without end (purpose), yet there is no striving. Nothing is without meaning, yet there is peaceful emptiness. Nothing is sought, yet all is provided in abundance. Jesus said: "Seek ye the kingdom of God and all these things shall be added unto you."[42] If we do not see beyond our limitations, we are confined to a mundane existence. There is nothing in the human condition itself that requires us to transcend these limitations. We can hypostatize the negativity of finiteness and see our life as an absurdity and a fraud. Or by accepting infinite Being as the source of our being, we can *denegate* our negativity and, realizing a coincidence of opposites, regain the basic affirmation of our being. This is not a state of idealism. It is not *in spite of* our limitations that we accept ourselves, but *even with* these limitations we enter the dimensionless dimension.

Whether one unites with the Transcendent by means of a mystical experience or through love, the characteristic that proceeds from it is the power to concentrate the content of one's life and the significance of reality in one single wish - to be a friend to God and to accept all others, knowing that God makes the rain to fall on the just and the unjust. Kierkegaard calls this "infinite resignation" since, for the enlightened, it is God who has persuasive power. Since we live in-the-world, we must find our life here, yet without losing the eternality we gain in uniting with the Transcendent.

We affirm our being through love. It is from Infinite Love that we receive our being and it is to Infinite Love that we return. It is by expressing our love to God that we communicate with him and realize our unity with all of being. He who loves all beings in God becomes one with God. Since it is with the motivation that God has given us that we are able to love Him, we can, by expressing our love to Him, know that by the same act He is loving us.

> God is love and he that dwelleth in love
> dwelleth in God, and God in him.[43]

1. Heidegger, *Being and Time*, p. 294

2. James M. Demske, *Being, Man, and Death* (Lexington: The University Press of Kentucky, 1970), p. 164

3. Heidegger, *Being and Time*, p. 307

4. Søren Kierkegaard, *Fear and Trembling and Sickness unto Death*, trans. W.Lowrie (Princeton: Princeton University Press, 1954), p. 53

5. Karlis Osis and Erlendur Haraldsson, *At the Hour of Death* (New York: Avon Books, 1977)

6. Sir James George Frazer, *The New Golden Bough*, ed. T. H. Gaster (New York: Criterion Books, 1959), p. 150

7. Ibid., p. 151

8. Ibid.

9. Plato, "Phaedo," *The Collected Dialogues*, 106e

10. Thomas Aquinas, *Summa Contra Gentiles* II, 79, 5

11. Nicolas Berdyaev, *The Destiny of Man* (New York: Harper & Row, 1960), p. 290

12. Ibid., p. 263

13. William James, "The Will to Believe," *Essays on Faith and Morals*, ed. R. B. Perry (New York: World Publishing, 1968), p. 34

14. Ibid, p. 50

15. Ibid., p. 55

16. Ludwig Wittgenstein, *Tractatus Logico-Philosophicus*, trans. D. F. Pears and B. F. McGuinness (London: Routledge & Kegan Paul, 1961), p. 151

17. Seng-t'san, Third Chinese Patriarch, "On Trust in the Heart," Christmas Humphreys, *Zen: A Way of Life* (New York: Emerson Books, 1965), p. 128

18. Huang Po, "The Wang Ling Record," John Blofeld, *The Zen Teaching of Huang Po on the Transmission of Mind* (New York: Grove Press, 1958), p.108

19. Suzuki, *Zen Doctrine of No-Mind*, p. 55

20. Joseph Maréchal, *Studies in the Psychology of the Mystics*, trans. A. Thorold (Albany, New York: Magi Books, 1964), p. 101

21. Karl Jaspers, *Way to Wisdom* (New Haven: Yale University Press, 1951), pp. 45 and 65

22. Wittgenstein, *Tractatus*, pp. 149-151

23. The commandments of Buddhism are: Do not destroy life; Do not steal; Do not commit an unchaste act; Do not lie; Do not take intoxicating liquor; Do not report the wrong doings of others; Do not slander another by praising yourself; Do not covet; Do not be stirred to anger; Do not revile the Three Treasures (which are: to surrender oneself to, to return to, and to rely on *That*)

24. Garma C. C. Chang, *The Practice of Zen* (New York: Harper & Row, 1959), p. 98

25. Hui-neng, "The Altar Sutra," in Lu K'uan Yu, *Ch'an and Zen Teaching* (London: Rider, 1961), III, 46

26. Matthew 5, 37

27. Blofeld, *Zen Teaching of Huang Po*, p. 80

28. Chang, *Practice of Zen*, p. 160. "The Mahamudra is called the 'Zen Buddhism of Tibet'...."

29. Hui-neng, "The Sutra of Hui-neng," In Daisetz Suzuki, *The Zen Doctrine of No-Mind* (London: Rider, 1969), p. 27

30. Christmas Humphreys, *Zen, a Way of Life* (New York: Emerson Books, 1965), p. 100

31. Hakuin Ekaku, "Monkey," from Isshu Miura and Ruth Fuller Sasaki, *The Zen Koan* (New York: Harcourt, Brace and World, 1965), unpaginated

32. St. John 14, 20

33. Bragdon, *The Eternal Poles*, pp. 94-95

34. Chang, *Practice of Zen*, p. 97

35. Ibid., p. 117

36. Said by Master Han Shan, Ibid., p. 139

37. Huang Po, "Chun Chow Record," Ibid., p. 36

38. Joseph Maréchal, *Studies in the Psychology of the Mystics*, trans. A. Thorold (Albany, N.Y.: Magi Books, 1964), p. 193

39. Blofeld, *Zen Teaching of Huang Po*, p. 79

40. Huang Po, "The Wan Ling Record," Ibid., p. 93

41. Isshu Miura & Ruth Fuller Sasaki, *The Zen Koan*, (New York: Harcourt, Brace, & World, 1965), unpaginated

42. St. Luke 12:31

43. I John 4, 16

BIBLIOGRAPHY

Adamczewski, Zygmunt. "Questions in Heidegger's Thought about Being," from *The Question of Being*. University Park: Pennsylvania State University Press, 1978.

Aquinas, Thomas. *The Disputed Questions on Truth*. Trans. from the definitive Leonine Text by R. W. Mulligan, S. J. 3 vols. Chicago: Henry Regnery, 1952.

.... *Scriptum super Libros Sententiarum Magistri Petri Lombardi*. 2 vols. Paris: Sumptibus P. Lethielleux, 1929.

.... *Summa Theologica*. 5 vols. Madrid: Biblioteca de Autores Cristianos, 1951.

Aristotle. *The Basic Works of Aristotle*. Ed. R. McKeon. New York: Random House, 1941.

Arnheim, Rudolf. *Visual Thinking*. Berkeley: University of California Press, 1969.

Beitzinger, A. J. "Hume's Aristocratic Preference." *Review of Politics*. Vol. 28 #2, Apr., 1966.

Benoit, Hubert. *The Supreme Doctrine*. New York: Viking Press, 1955.

Berdyaev, Nicolas. *The Destiny of Man*. New York: Harper & Row, 1960.

Bergson, Henri. *Time and Free Will*. Ed. F. L. Pogson. New York: Harper & Row, 1960.

Berkeley, George. *Berkeley, Essays, Principles, Dialogues*. New York: Charles Scribner's Sons, 1957.

Berkeley, George. *A Treatise Concerning the Principles of Human Knowledge,* Ed. T. E. Jessop, *The Works of George Berkeley.* Vol. II. London: Thomas Nelson & Sons, 1964.

.... *Three Dialogues Between Hylas and Philonous.* Ed. T. E. Jessop. Berkeley, George. *The Works of George Berkeley.* Ed. A. A. Luce and T. E. Jessop. London: Thomas Nelson and Sons, 1964. Vol. II.

.... *The Principles of Human Knowledge.* Ed. T. E. Jessop. *The Works of George Berkeley.* Vol. II.

Binswanger, Ludwig. *Being-in-the-World.* Trans. J. Needleman. New York: Harper & Row, 1963.

.... *Existence.* Ed. R. May, E. Angel and H. F. Ellenberger. New York: Basic Books, 1958.

Blofeld, John, trans. *The Zen Teaching of Huang Po on the Transmission of Mind.* New York: Grove Press, 1958.

.... trans. *The Zen Teaching of Hui Hai on Sudden Illumination.* London: Rider, 1969.

Bragdon, Claude. *The Eternal Poles.* New York: Alfred A. Knopf, 1931.

Buber, Martin. *I and Thou.* Trans. R. G. Smith. New York: Scribner Son's, 1958.

Buscaglia, Leo. *Living, Loving & Learning.* Ed. Steven Short. New York: Holt Rinehart & Winston, 1982.

Chan, Wing-Tsit, trans. *A Source Book in Chinese Philosophy.* Princeton: Princeton University Press, 1963.

Chang, Garma C. C. *The Practice of Zen*. New York: Harper & Row, 1959.

Collins, James. *God in Modern Philosophy*. Chicago: Henry Regnery, 1959.

.... *A History of Modern European Philosophy*. Milwaukee: Bruce Publishing, 1961.

Crick, Francis. *Of Molecules and Men*. Seattle: University of Washington Press, 1966.

Croce, Benedetto. *Aesthetic*. Trans. Douglas Ainislie. New York: The Noonday Press, 1956.

Demske, James M. *Being, Man, and Death*. Lexington: The University Press of Kentucky, 1970.

Frankl, Viktor. *Man's Search for Meaning*. Trans. I. Lasch. New York: Simon & Schuster, 1959.

Frazier, Sir James. *The New Golden Bough*. Ed. T. H. Gautier. New York: Criterion Books, 1959.

Freud, Sigmund. *The Ego and the Id*. Trans. J. Riviere, ed. J. Strachey. New York: W. W. Norton, 1960.

Goldstein, Kurt. *Human Nature in the Light of Psychopathology*. Cambridge, Massachusetts: Harvard University Press, 1940.

Goldstein, Kurt and Scheerer, Martin. *Abstract and Concrete Behavior: Psychological Monographs*. Ed. J. F. Dashiell. Evanston, Illinois: *The American Psychological Association*, 1941. Vol. 53 #2.

Gould, Thomas. *Platonic Love*. New York: Free Press of Glencoe, 1963.

Guitton, Jean. *Human Love*. Chicago: Franciscan Herald Press, 1966.

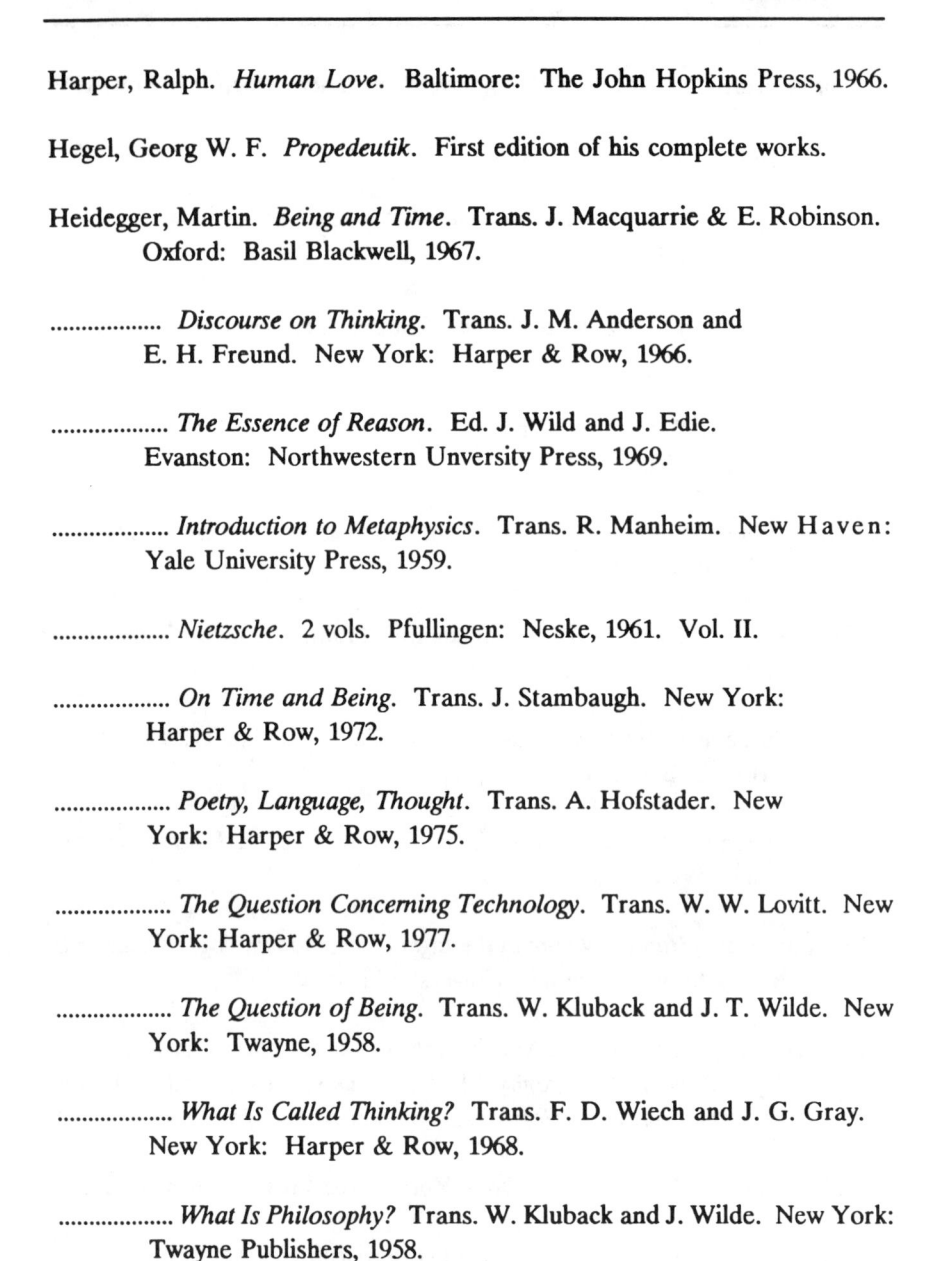

Harper, Ralph. *Human Love*. Baltimore: The John Hopkins Press, 1966.

Hegel, Georg W. F. *Propedeutik*. First edition of his complete works.

Heidegger, Martin. *Being and Time*. Trans. J. Macquarrie & E. Robinson. Oxford: Basil Blackwell, 1967.

.... *Discourse on Thinking*. Trans. J. M. Anderson and E. H. Freund. New York: Harper & Row, 1966.

.... *The Essence of Reason*. Ed. J. Wild and J. Edie. Evanston: Northwestern Unversity Press, 1969.

.... *Introduction to Metaphysics*. Trans. R. Manheim. New Haven: Yale University Press, 1959.

.... *Nietzsche*. 2 vols. Pfullingen: Neske, 1961. Vol. II.

.... *On Time and Being*. Trans. J. Stambaugh. New York: Harper & Row, 1972.

.... *Poetry, Language, Thought*. Trans. A. Hofstader. New York: Harper & Row, 1975.

.... *The Question Concerning Technology*. Trans. W. W. Lovitt. New York: Harper & Row, 1977.

.... *The Question of Being*. Trans. W. Kluback and J. T. Wilde. New York: Twayne, 1958.

.... *What Is Called Thinking?* Trans. F. D. Wiech and J. G. Gray. New York: Harper & Row, 1968.

.... *What Is Philosophy?* Trans. W. Kluback and J. Wilde. New York: Twayne Publishers, 1958.

Heisenberg, Werner. *Physics and Philosophy.* New York: Harper & Row, 1958.

Horney, Karen. *The Neurotic Personality of Our Time.* New York: W. W. Norton, 1964.

Huizinga, Johan. *Homo Ludens.* Boston: Beacon Press, 1950.

Hume, David. *The Essential Works of David Hume.* Ed. R. Cohen. New York: Bantam Books, 1965.

.... *Philosophical Works,* Ed. T. H. Green and T. H. Grose. 4 Vols. London: Scientia Verlag Aalen, 1964.

Humphreys, Christmas. *Zen: A Way of Life.* New York: Emerson Books, 1965.

James, William. *Essays on Faith and Morals.* Ed. R. B. Perry. New York: World Publishing, 1968.

.... *Pragmatism. The works of William James.* Cambridge: Harvard University Press, 1979.

.... *Psychology: Briefer Course.* New York: Collier Books, 1962.

.... *The Varieties of Mystical Experience.* New York: Collier Books, 1961.

Jaspers, Karl. *Man in the Modern Age.* Trans. E. Paul and C. Paul. London: Routledge & Kegan Paul, 1966).

.... *Way to Wisdom.* New Haven: Yale University Press, 1951.

Johann, Robert, S.J. *The Meaning of Love.* Glen Rock, New Jersey: Paulist Press, 1966.

Jung, Carl. *Civilization in Transition. The Collected Works of C. G. Jung.* Trans. R. Hull. Vol. X. New York: Pantheon Books, 1964.

.... *The Collected Works of C. G. Jung.* Trans. R. F. C. Hull. 10 vols. New York: Pantheon Books, 1964. Vol. X.

.... *Psyche and Symbol.* Ed. V. S. de Laszlo. Garden City, New York: Doubleday, 1958.

Kahn, Charles H. "Linguistic Relativism and the Greek Project of Ontology." *The Question of Being.* Ed. M. Sprung. University Park, Pennsylvania: Pennsylvania State University Press, 1978.

Kierkegaard, Søren. *Fear and Trembling* and *The Sickness unto Death.* Trans. W. Lowrie. Princeton: Princeton University Press, 1954.

Kostelanetz, Richard, ed. *Aesthetics Contemporary.* Buffalo, N.Y.: Prometheus Books, 1978.

Lonergan, Bernard J.F. *Insight.* New York: Harper & Row, 1978.

Luijpen, William A. *Existential Phenomenology.* Pittsburgh: Duquesne University Press, 1965.

Marcel, Gabriel. *Being and Having.* Trans. K. Farrer. New York: Harper & Row, 1965.

.... *Homo Viator.* Trans. E. Crauford. Gloucester, Mass.: Peter Smith, 1978.

Maréchal, Joseph. *Studies in the Psychology of the Mystics.* Trans. A. Thorold. lbany, New York: Magi Books, 1964.

Maslow, Abraham. "Love in Healthy People." *The Practice of Love.* Ed. A. Montague. Englewood Cliffs, New Jersey: Prentice Hall, 1975.

May, Rollo. *The Courage to Create*. New York: W. W. Norton, 1976.

---------- *Love and Will*. New York: W. W. Norton, 1967.

---------- *Psychology and the Human Dilemna*. New York: D. Van Nostrand, 1967.

McLean, George, ed. *The Human Person*. Proceedings of the American Catholic Philosophical Association, Vol. LIII, 1979.

Merleau-Ponty, Maurice. *Phenomenology of Perception*. London: Routledge & Kegan Paul, 1965.

Milgram, Stanley. *Obedience to Authority*. New York: Harper & Row, 1969.

Miura, Isshu and Ruth Fuller Sasaki. *The Zen Koan*. New York: Harcourt, Brace and World, 1965.

Montagu, Ashley, ed. *The Practice of Love*. Englewood Cliffs, New Jersey: Prentice Hall, 1974.

Morowitz, Harold J. "Rediscovering the Mind." *Psychology Today*. August, 1980, Vol. 14 #3.

Mouroux, Jean. *The Meaning of Man*. Trans. A. H. G. Downes. Garden City, New York: Doubleday, 1961.

Murray, Michael, ed. *Heidegger and Modern Philosophy*. New Haven: Yale University Press, 1978.

Neal, Helen. "The Spinal Gate Theory of Pain." *American Pharmacy*. Vol. N. S. 18 #12, Nov., 1978.

Nédoncelle, Maurice. *Love and the Person*. Trans. R. Adelaide. New York: Sheed & Ward, 1966.

O'Brien, Elmer, S. J. *Varieties of Mystical Experience.* New York: Holt, Rhinehart & Winston, 1964.

Osis, Karlis and Erlendur Haraldsson. *At the Hour of Death.* New York: Avon Books, 1977.

Piaget, Jean. *The Child's Conception of Number.* New York: W. W. Norton, 1965.

.... *The Construction of Reality in the Child.* Trans. M. Cook. New York: Basic Books, 1954.

.... *Play, Dreams, and Imitation in Childhood.* Trans. C. Gattegno and F. M. Hodgson. New York: W. W. Norton, 1951.

Phillips, Jr., John L. *The Origins of Intellect, Piaget's Theory.* San Francisco: W. H. Freeman, 1969.

Pinchot, Roy B. ed. *The Human Body.* Washington, D.C.: U.S. News Books, 1981.

Plato. "Phaedo." *The Collected Dialogues.* 106e.

.... "Republic." *The Collected Works of Plato.* Trans. E. Hamilton and H. Cairns. New York: Pantheon Books, 1941, Vol. VI.

Rensberger, Boyce. "Talking Chimpanzee Asks for Names of Things Now." *New York Times*, Dec. 4, 1974.

Ricoeur, Paul. "The Task of Hermeneutics." *Heidegger and Modern Philosophy.* Ed. M. Murray. New Haven: Yale University Press, 1978

.... *The Symbolism of Evil.* Trans. E. Buchanan. Boston: Beacon Press, 1969.

Bibliography

Ross, Stephen David, ed. *An Anthology of Aesthetic Theory*. Albany: State University of New York, 1984.

Rukavina, Thomas J. "Heidegger's Theory of Being." *The New Scholasticism*. Vol. XL, #4, Oct., 1966.

Sadler, William A. *Existence and Love*. New York: Charles Scribner, 1969.

Sartre, Jean-Paul. *Being and Nothingness*. Trans. H. E. Barnes. New York: Philosophical Library, 1956.

Scheler, Max. *The Nature of Sympathy*. Trans. P. Heath. London: Routledge & Kegan Paul, 1970.

Sophocles. "Antigone." *The Complete Greek Tragedies*. Ed. D. Gren and R. Lattimore. Chicago: University of Chicago Press, 1957.

Sorokin, Pitirim. *The Ways and Power of Love*. Chicago: Henry Regnery, 1965.

Spinoza, Benedict de. "Ethics," IV, prop. 4, *Chief Works of Benedict de Spinoza*. Trans. R. H. M Elwes. London: Bell & Sons, 1919.

Sprung, Mervyn, ed. *The Question of Being, East-West Perspectives*. University Park: Pennsylvania State University Press, 1978.

Steger, E. Ecker. "The No-Philosophy of Zen." *The Personalist*. Vol. LV #3, Summer, 1974.

──────── "Verbum Cordis." *Divus Thomas*. Piacenza: Colegio Alberoni, 1978. Vol. 81 #16.

Suzuki, Daisetz. *Studies in Zen*. Ed. C. Humphreys. New York: Delta, 1955.

Suzuki, Daisetz. *Zen Buddhism*. Ed. W. Barrett. Garden City, New York: Doubleday Anchor, 1956.

ـــــــــــ *The Zen Doctrine of No-Mind*. Ed. C. Humphreys. London: Rider, 1969.

Tillich, Paul. *The Courage to Be*. New Haven: Yale University Press, 1952.

ـــــــــــ *Love, Power, and Justice*. Oxford: Oxford University Press, 1960.

Time Magazine. "Behavior Mod Behind the Walls: Use on Prisoners." March 11, 1974.

Wei Wu Wei. *Ask the Awakened*. London: Routledge & Kegan Paul, 1963).

Wild, John. *The Radical Empiricism of William James*. Garden City, New York: Doubleday, 1969.

Wittgenstein, Ludwig. *Tractatus Logico-Philosophicus*. Trans. D. F. Pears and B. F. McGuinness. London: Routledge & Kegan Paul, 1961.

Yü, Lu K'uan. *Ch'an and Zen Teaching*. London: Rider, 1961. III.

Zukav, Gary. *The Dancing Wu Li Masters, An Overview of the New Physics*. New York: William Morrow, 1979.

INDEX

abstraction 18-21, 65, 78
anima/animus 143-145
artwork 129-132
Aristotle 29, 146
authenticity 126
axioms 16-22
being 5-7, 25-26, 72-74, 77, 80, 94, 97, 107
Being-in-totality 6, 80, 103, 105, 131
Being itself, infinite Being 6, 54, 102, 174ff
Berdyaev 171
Bergson 1-2
Berkeley (see Contents for Immaterialism) 13-15
Binswanger 159
body 52-54
brain 46ff
Buber 139-140
call of conscience 125-126
causality 24, 43-44, 92-94, 102
collective unconscious 29ff, 143-145
concern 103
conscience 125-126
contemporary philosophy (see Contents)
courage 126, 158
creativity (see Contents for Chap.V) 128-131, 133-134
Dasein 5, 25-26
death 167-168
Descartes 22, 26
difference of degree and kind 16-22
dream 29ff
ecstasy 183-185
emotion 77, 148-149
empathy 26-27
enlightenment 179ff

esse   23-24
essence   23
eternal life   168ff
ethical   121-122
Frankl   120
freedom (see Contents for Chapter V) 177-178
Freud   12, 30, 112, 141
Goldstein   73-74, 78
guilt   123-125
Heidegger (see Contents for Contemporary Philosophy)   1-2, 25, 167-168, 175
Hobbes   97
Horney   155-156, 158
Hume (see Contents for Materialism)   10
Idealism (see Immaterialism)
imagination   41-43
immaterialism (See Contents)
immortality   168ff
intellectual power (see Contents for Chapter III) 67ff
intellectual word   70, 121
James, William 2, 11-13, 36, 59, 77, 88-90, 172-173
Jaspers   156, 159, 177
Jung   29ff, 123, 128, 143-145, 155
justice   95-97, 121
kind, difference of 19-22
love (see Contents for Chap.V)
Luijpen   52-54, 152
Marcel   32-34, 52
Marèchal   177-178
mask   32-34
Maslow   149
materialism (see Contents)
May, Rollo   128, 140, 155
Melzack-Wall Spinal Gate Theory 51
Milgrim Experiment 116-118

Index

mood 77, 83, 106
Multiple Me's 11-13, 36
necessary connection 40-41
Nêdoncelle 154
optimism 99-100, 158
Peirce 2
pessimism 94-95, 158
philosophical anthropology 1-4, 39
physicomorphic fallacy 2
Piaget 54-59, 132
Plato 65, 143, 169-170
play 131-133
Prajña 184
presuppositions (see Summaries of Chapter I-VI)
reductionism 2-3
rights 96-97, 121
romantic Love 143-144
St. Paul 162
St. Thomas Aquinas (see Contents for Traditional Philosophy) 120-121, 146-149, 170-171,
Sartre 27-28
Satori 183ff
Scapegoatism 123-124
Scheler 153
science 2-3
self (see Chapter I)
self-integration 29ff, 144-145
self-reflection 68-69, 118
sense image, production of: 45ff
senses (see Contents) 16-17, 67, 71-76, 82-83, 91-92
Skinner 3, 95
Sorokin 160-161
stream of consciousness 11
Sunyata 179ff
Suzuki 3

Taoism   100-101
tender and tough/minded 88-89
the *they* of publicness   79-80
thrownness   105
traditional philosophy (see Contents)
transcendence   7, 80, 121
truth   65-67, 70, 77-78, 83
understanding (see Contents for Chapter III)
unity   22-24
values   119-122
will power   58-59, 118ff, 122
Wittgenstein   174, 178
world (see Contents for Chapter IV) 153
Yogacara   98-99
Zen Buddhism (see also Hui-Neng)   179-185